IT'S NOT EASY BEING GREEN

IT'S NOT EASY BEING GREEN

Text by Ken Yeang

Book Design and Art by Tuck Leong

ORO
EDITIONS

Publishers of Architecture, Art, and Design
Gordon Goff: Publisher

www.oroeditions.com
info@oroeditions.com

Published by ORO Editions

Book Design and Art by Tuck Leong
Text by: Ken Yeang
Managing Editor: Jake Anderson

10 9 8 7 6 5 4 3 2 1 First Edition

ISBN: 978-1-939621-86-3

Color Separations and Printing: ORO Group Ltd.
Printed in China.

International Distribution: www.oroeditions.com/distribution

ORO Editions makes a continuous effort to minimize the overall carbon footprint of its publications. As part of this goal, ORO Editions, in association with Global ReLeaf, arranges to plant trees to replace those used in the manufacturing of the paper produced for its books. Global ReLeaf is an international campaign run by American Forests, one of the world's oldest nonprofit conservation organizations. Global ReLeaf is American Forests' education and action program that helps individuals, organizations, agencies, and corporations improve the local and global environment by planting and caring for trees.

TABLE OF CONTENTS

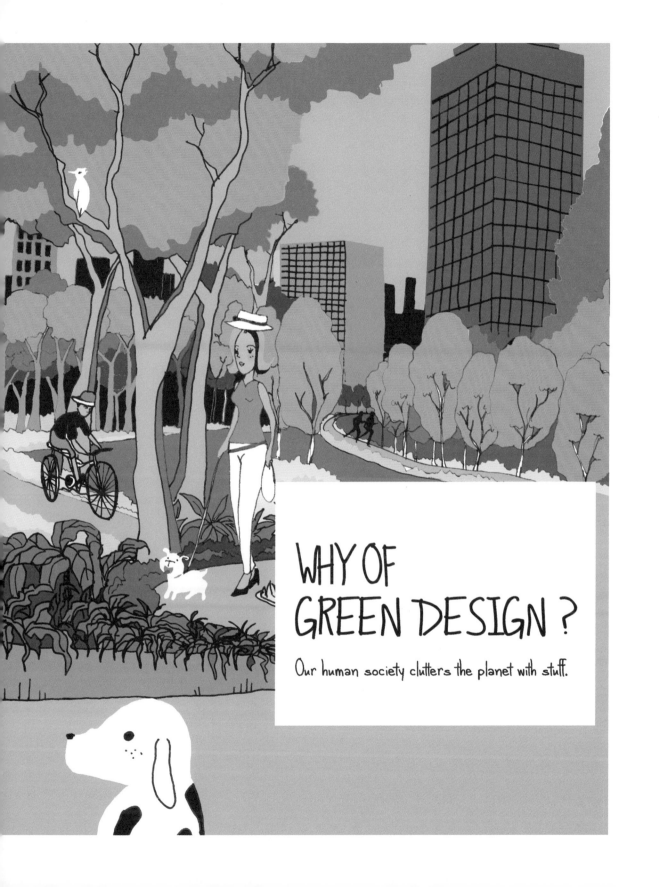

WHY OF
GREEN DESIGN ?

Our human society clutters the planet with stuff.

Society's export-driven economies and their industrial manufacturing systems produce a multitude of artifacts and products (including large items such as cars, trucks, electronic goods, white goods, food products, etc,) in

In effect, humans make significantly more artifacts than any other species in nature. Additionally, the emissions from its energy production systems pollute the biosphere's biogeochemical cycles and are changing global climate for the worse.

Humans make more things than any other species in nature and their extensive construction of large clusters of urban structures, such as towns and cities linked by networks of highways and massive interchanges, are, in totality, turning the planet into a single constructed artifact.

It is the environmentally-callousness of these production, in its unfettered use and WANTON DISPOSAL in an existent "through-put flow", that is the root cause of the present day's state of environmental impairment. Even if we halt all present local and global human acts of environmental impairment, the decline already set in motion will continue well into the future. If we do not take concerted action now

THIS MILLENNIUM COULD WELL BE OUR LAST.

But, what if we anticipate this impairment in the early stages of design and design the new built environment to avert its negative environmental consequences in order to **achieve zero impact** and positive outcomes before execution? What if, in this trajectory, we also redesign the existing artifacts to **rectify their negative consequences?**

What if, in design, we anticipate where the constructed and manufactured products will go at the end of their useful life, and design to enable their environmentally-benign disassembly for reuse, recycling, reconstitution, and their eventually seamless assimilation **back into the natural environment?**

In answer to the question,

"WHY GREEN DESIGN?"

The answer is simple —

It's the right thing to do.

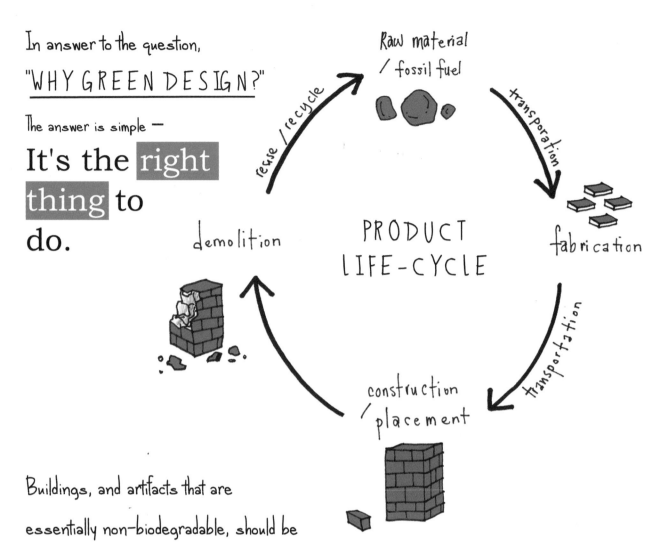

Raw material / fossil fuel

reuse/recycle

transportation

PRODUCT LIFE-CYCLE

demolition

fabrication

transportation

construction / placement

Buildings, and artifacts that are essentially non-biodegradable, should be produced only after we have DESIGNED INTO THEM their projected life-cycle: from the time that the raw materials are extracted, to their production and fabrication, and, finally, to what happens to them at the end of their useful life. We need to consider how materials at the end of this flow could be addressed. We need to design the product or artifact's afterlife from the outset rather than after production. We need to eliminate the question of their disposal inasmuch as possible.

" This anticipatory design approach is the fundamental objective of **ECODESIGN** . Effectively achieving this goal is the challenge of green design. The recognition of the significance of this will have far reaching implications for designers in their approach to design. "

Likely, at some tipping point in our society's future, or, perhaps more imminent, when society's global environmental impairment goes beyond the planet's carrying capacity and the global ecosystems collapse, all of society will start questioning the causes and arrive at the same conclusion:

environmental impairment could have been averted if only we had started by designing away these consequences instead of seeking to rectify them in catch-up-mode.

When society and the design community question and recognize this apparent deficiency in our existent design approach and our production systems the widespread response will be a <u>demand to radically redesign</u> and remake all our artifacts and our energy, industrial, and agricultural production systems.

This will lead to the widespread re-manufacturing, re-production and re-fabrication of everything that we make – our artifacts, built systems, and their processes, including the retrofitting of existing ones.

ACIDIC CONTAMINANTS POLLUTANTS ARTIFICIALS NON-RENEWABLE TOXIC BUILT SYSTEM

ZERO-CARBON NATURE ORGANIC RECYCLE RENEWABLE ZERO WASTE BIODEGRADABLE GREEN

Green designing, by which time, becomes no longer an option but

A NECESSITY.

The key issue is that we should not wait for this tipping point to take concerted action.

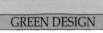

GREEN DESIGN

Unfortunately most of our current designers—the present generation of architects, engineers, planners, industrial designers, and all whose work impinges on the natural environment — are not literate in ecology and environmental sciences.

Most are ignorant of the environmental consequences of their ACTIONS & DECISIONS at the local ecosystem level and at the bioregional and greater biosphere level.

Prior to this task of redesigning the global community of designers need to be RE-EDUCATED in ecology.

This does not just apply to those already in practice but to the future generation of designers — our students. The schools of design must now teach

ecology, how it influences design, and how design affects the ecology of the environment.

This will enable the students to see their designed outcomes from the eyes of

a naturalist and not just as artists or craftspeople. They should not regard their designed products as simply

commercial items or social enterprises, but as vital and integral parts of nature.

It is this rationale that drives my work in

ecoarchitecture.

01 EARLY EXPERIENCE IN ARCHITECTURE

I became interested in ecology only later in my mid-twenties, but I first became intrigued

with architecture at an early age of four when I accompanied my father, a medical doctor,

on his regular visits to a construction site where he was

having a house built for my mother. It was in the early

'50s. The large house was a white house in a modernist

style with **Frank Lloyd Wright**

aesthetics, designed by the locally celebrated Dutch

architect Berthold Iverson, a resident of Ipoh, Malaysia.

This was my first introduction to architecture and building – walking through the construction site with my Dad, stepping, occasionally painfully, on the timber formwork with protruding nails, watching steel reinforcements being laid in place for the ground beams, and the pouring of concrete. I instantly liked the idea of making things as a craft, especially very large structures, This early, vivid experience put the seed of being an ARCHITECT in my head.

My interest in design developed when I entered <u>Cheltenham College</u> at 12. This was a strict British boarding school with a strong military emphasis where the cadet corps training was taken seriously.

The school was in Gloucestershire where the Gloucester Regiment was based, with many of its retired military personnel still living in the county. At Cheltenham, I spent most of my free afternoons at the art studio painting and making art objects.

I found the college buildings – its massive chapel, grand dining hall, assembly hall, the classroom block, and the gym –

incredibly **DREARY & UGLY**. These were built in beige sandstone in a classical <u>Victorian style</u>. The only pleasurable place is the quadrangle at its center, with a semi-covered walkway to one side where people posted events and exam results on notice boards.

CHELTENHAM

LONDON

Visiting London during the holidays, I encountered even more uninspiring, ugly and mostly old buildings. Many of the new office buildings and schools were rapidly built prefab structures. There were the occasional new, massive structures and major cultural buildings, many in "off-form" concrete **"Beton Brut"** or **"Brutalist"** style, being the flavor of the day, after Le Corbusier.

I did not understand why modern
architecture had to be so boring, unfriendly,
joyless, and aesthetically dull, whereas,
I found the exciting architecture to be
the multi-coloured shop-fronts on
Carnaby Street and Kings Road.

This was Britain in the '60s – the **"Buy Britain"** years. I wondered why the city's
architecture could not be similarly fun and joyful? Surely this is the incredible purpose and
power of architecture, to give joy and pleasure to all who use it.

The aesthetic influences of the day were a Britain at its apotheosis. It was the '60s with the trendy colorful designs of Peter Max, the Yellow Submarine, of Mary Quant's fashion, Jeff Banks' flower-power shirts, bell-bottom trousers, zip-up boots and black, roll-neck shirts (both influenced by the Beatles). In the background was the ongoing conflict between the "Mods" and the "Rockers" (a myth promoted by the press), Antonioni's film "Blow Up" with David Hemmings, and, architecturally, for me it was the transformative colorful graphics in the "Dan Dare" comics-style of drawing and the "plug-in" architecture of the Archigram architects group at the AA (Architectural Association) School in London.

PEACE!

I did not follow in my father's footsteps to be a medical doctor.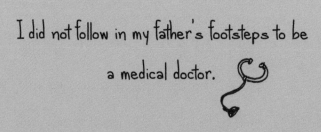

I eventually agreed with my parents to study architecture instead of art, which was my first choice. I was influenced in part by my uncles who were architects and developers in London.

Upon finishing my A-levels at Cheltenham, I sought to enter the AA School while still in my late teens. At 17, I was the youngest at the AA's 1st year students.

My architectural training at the AA School was the **TURNING POINT** . The AA was a liberal school where a form of student anarchy was its zeitgeist. The school was regarded as a maverick institution with a strong experimental design reputation, often described in the journals as a "hot-house of ideas" having a laissez-faire approach to teaching and supervision.

It was a liberating and thrilling time at this stage of my life and, of course, the instant **FREEDOM** was a startling change from my earlier regimented life at the strict boarding school wearing double-breasted reefer jacket with grey flannel trousers and tasseled mortar-board hats, of rugby and cricket, to a liberal and permissive environment. From my first day at the AA's 1st year studio, I knew architecture was what I wanted to do for the rest of my life.

I first learnt about contemporary architecture and about Modernism from my 1st year master, Elia Zenghelis, later a founder of OMA with Rem Koolhaas. The first lecture I attended was on Panofsky (Erwin) on "classicalism" delivered by the critic and originator of "post-modernism" architecture

Charles Jencks, who later became a friend. It was during my middle years at the AA that I met Tengku Robert Hamzah, a prince from the Kelantan Malay royal family who I became business partners with in 1975 when I returned to Malaysia.

LETS' DO THIS!

After my 3rd year of studies, in 1969, I left London for Singapore to intern for a year with my Father's architect, Stanley Leong, who was designing a beachfront hotel for my Father in Penang.

I worked first as a junior draftsman at the construction site office for the Singapore Mandarin Hotel, doing drawing construction details. My final internship months were spent back at the company's head office where the main staff of five was. It was there that I learned the most about architectural practice and acquired enormous professional experience, tPermitted to take on the role of an assistant architect on a variety of projects, I did just about the entire gamut of an architect's scope of work, guided by M.Y. Chang, the Chief Draftsman. After this period of intensive internship, I returned to London to complete my studies towards my AA diploma.

From that moment I decided to go through my architectural studies in haste. More than just being youthfully full of myself and extremely impatient, I sought to do my 5th year's portfolio exams right at the beginning of my 4th year.

That winter was UK's "winter of discontent" with a national power grid strike under the Labour premiership of Harold Wilson. I was furiously drafting without electricity, with two candles mounted at each end of my tee square and with my mother anxiously serving hot coffee.

I designed a small cinema in Kensington, then a large hospital in Milton Keynes, influenced by the ideas on indeterminate architecture of Lord Llewelyn Davies (whose firm I later became a brief share-holder in in 2005). I also designed a large mid-rise housing scheme for a large site at Land's End in Chelsea between King's Road and Cheyne Walk, opposite the "Granny Takes a Trip" boutique with the protruding truck facade. The residential units were designed based on the prevalent Parker Morris housing standards.

The same site was eventually developed and was designed in a Modernist style by Dennis Lasdun.

As part of the school's academic requirements, I had to write two essays – a history essay and a technical one. The topic for my history essay was the experimental Japanese Metaboist architect group (in 1971). It was fortuitous then that several years later I met one of its leading proponents, Kisho Kurokawa, in 1974, who I was introduced to over tea by Jencks. Kurokawa became an important mentor and also introduced me to Japan. My other mandatory technical essay was on "design methods", as a cybernetic reiterative process of

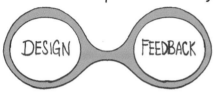

. The head of the AA's Technical Studies, John Starling insisted that I meet another student from the AA's Graduate School who had similar interests in design methods. The graduate student was the Turkish architect, Suha Ozkan, who later became the Secretary General of the Aga Khan Award for Architecture, and whom I met later in 1992 when I received an Aga Khan Award. The AA school was stunned when I passed the 5th year portfolio at the beginning of my 4th year. I still had a remaining year and a half education grant from my local Authority of Camden County Council. Footloose, I was on the lookout for a new field of venture.

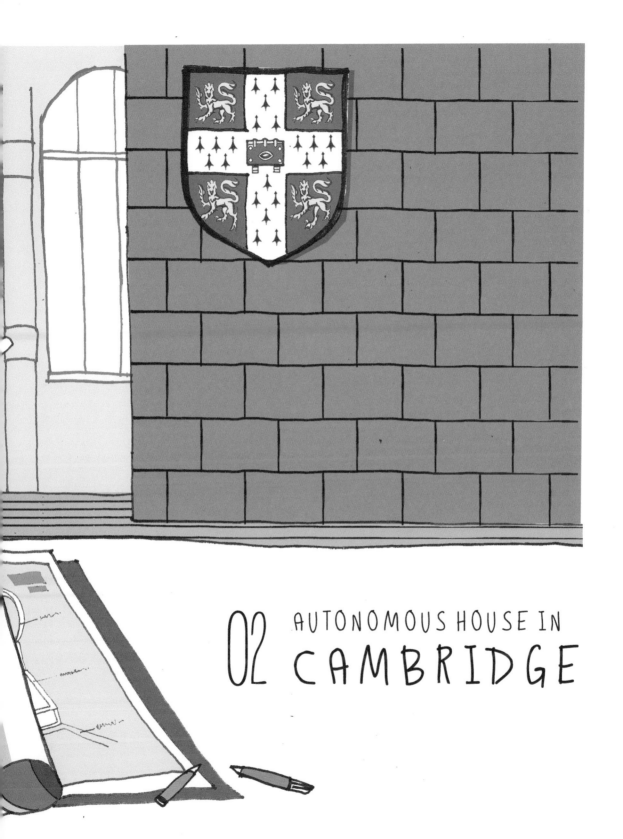

02 AUTONOMOUS HOUSE IN CAMBRIDGE

The idea of an ecoarchitecture emerged later, after I started research for a doctorate at Cambridge University. At that time in the early '70s, there was little work done in this field. Entry to Cambridge came soon after I met John Frazer, one evening at the AA's Members Room. Frazer, with Alex Pike— both lecturers at Cambridge University— were just embarking on setting up

their "Technical Research Division" at the University of Cambridge's Department of Architecture to research, design and build the **autonomous house**.

Frazer and Pike had received a large grant from the UK Government's Social Science Research Council to research and build the project. Frazer offered me a position as a research student with his team which I accepted. I left London for Cambridge in the Michaelmas term of 1971.

Cambridge is a university town. Life at Wolfson College was one of quiet research and writing, away from the chaos and competitiveness of London, mixing with the incredibly brilliant scholars from different faculties during mealtimes, and evenings with tutors and Fellows of other colleges. There were, of course, the May Balls, strangely held in April after the exams, with the punting to Grantchester afterwards at the end of each ball.

The **autonomous house project** was an idea mooted by the US inventor, engineer and visionary, Buckminster Fuller. The challenging proposition was to design and build a house that was <u>not connected to the city's utilities</u> – a dwelling with an independent electricity and water supply, and sewerage disposal and food production system.

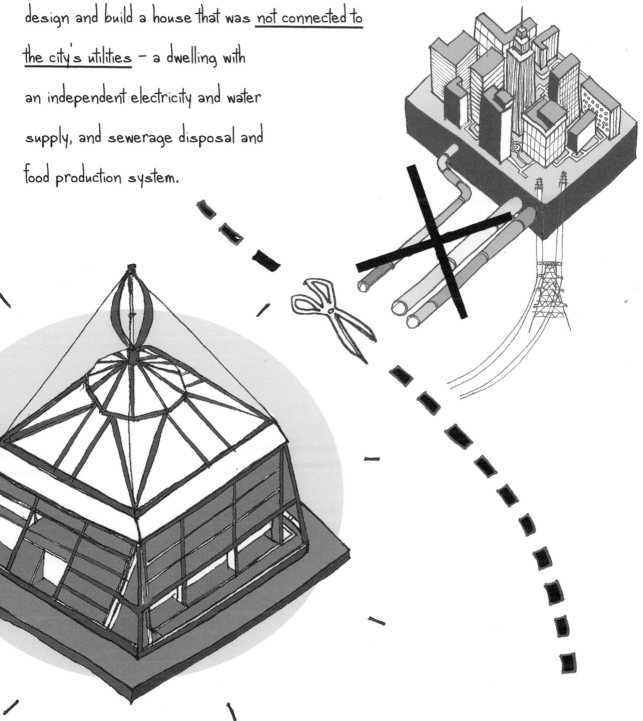

It was by then the early '70s and the earlier days of the student's revolution of the '60s,

of pot, <u>Woodstock and Ashbury Heights</u> were over.

This decade heralded a much more sober

mood with the beginning of the green

movement spurred by Rachel Carson's

famous book, "Silent Spring" (1962), which

was paralleled by the more formal and much

criticized systems-influenced Club of Rome's

"Limit to Growth" (1972), by the placard-carrying Ecologist magazine and Stewart Brand's clas-

sic counterculture tome, "The Whole Earth Catalogue" (1972).

However, this new environmental ethos was not wholeheartedly accepted by the British estab-

lishment nor by the engineering and architectural status quo. It was regarded with circumspect,

seen more as a **hippie** Luddite with preoccupation for commune living and farming in the

rural countryside.

Several months into the research work on the autonomous house project, I concluded that the team was essentially just working on engineering systems for a self-sufficient autarkic dwelling. While the engineering technologies for the house were technically feasible, they were, at that time, still

largely experimental. Technical support from the external professional engineering consultancies was simply non-existent, certainly unlike today when just about every M&E engineer professes expertise in sustainable engineering systems.

I questioned what the real issues underlying the autonomous house project were. What were the premises upon which the idea of the autonomous house was anchored? While I regarded the autonomous house project relevant as a useful endeavor toward findng answers to address our concerns for society's sustainable and resilient future, I believed that delving straight into the micro ecoengineering aspects to be premature.

" I believed that we should start by addressing the bigger picture, and that surely the focus should be on finding ways to design to reduce society's wastes and negative impacts on the environment, to create restorative and regenerative environments, and to design to redefine our human society's and built environment's relationship with the natural environment. "

While being aware of the environmental issues, I found that designers did not have a formal basis or a unified comprehensive approach for designing. The existent approach was incomplete and piecemeal. It was clear that designing for the natural environment had no place at the Technical Research Unit's program. I asked about the relationship of the project to the ecology of the environment? This was just politely ignored.

Ecology was not the focus of the unit. I contended that we cannot continue to design in the same way that we had been doing and that we need to design taking the natural environment into consideration and concluded that what we need was a basis for ecological design, which was missing in the autonomous house project.

The **real topic to me was essentially "ecological design."** It became evident that there was a dearth of work in looking at this overall view for designing for our sustainable future and that this was an area that needed urgent and vital research, and certainly, in any event, B E F O R E we sought to address the micro aspects in its ecoengineering.

03 RESEARCHING ECODESIGN

I sought leave from the Technical Research Unit

and the Faculty to work on "ecological design and planning" as the research topic of my doctorate.

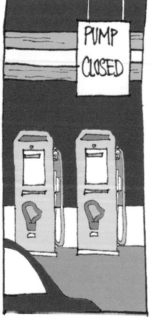

PUMP CLOSED

The **oil crisis** of 1973 gave impetus to my application. In researching the idea of an ecoarchitecture, it became apparent that our existent approach to design and planning needed to be R E T H O U G H T with natural environment being central to the making of a sustainable architecture.

<u>We need to change our view</u>, not just of architecture but our whole worldview of artifact making by society.

I attended lectures on ecology at the University's Department of Environmental Biology under Beament (J.W.L.). These studies changed my worldview of human society's relationship with nature and led me to join the British Ecological Society.

tree!

These studies led to the further study of the ecological land-use planning approach advanced by Ian McHarg at the Department of Landscape Architecture at the University of Pennsylvania and advanced ecological landscape architects elsewhere.

I received a travel grant to go attend McHarg's classes in Pennsylvania. There I found McHarg's work immensely relevant. In effect, it became the baseline and springboard for my research work.

Ian McHarg.
1920 - 2001

McHarg's land-use planning approach was based on the mapping of the ecological features of the place or region that is analysed using a LAYER-CAKE overlay and sieve-mapping technique to derive the basis for land-use zoning and layout planning.

I found the approach was essentially about masterplanning and it became evident that this was as far as McHarg's ecological planning approach could go, remaining at the level of site planning. I thought that it needed to transcend to architectural design where it was non-existent then. I believe McHarg had actually wanted to advance his ecological land-use planning approach to the next level — to take the approach to the realm of architectural design to enable architects to design an ecological architecture. I thought that McHarg was unable to achieve this, perhaps because he was not an architect.

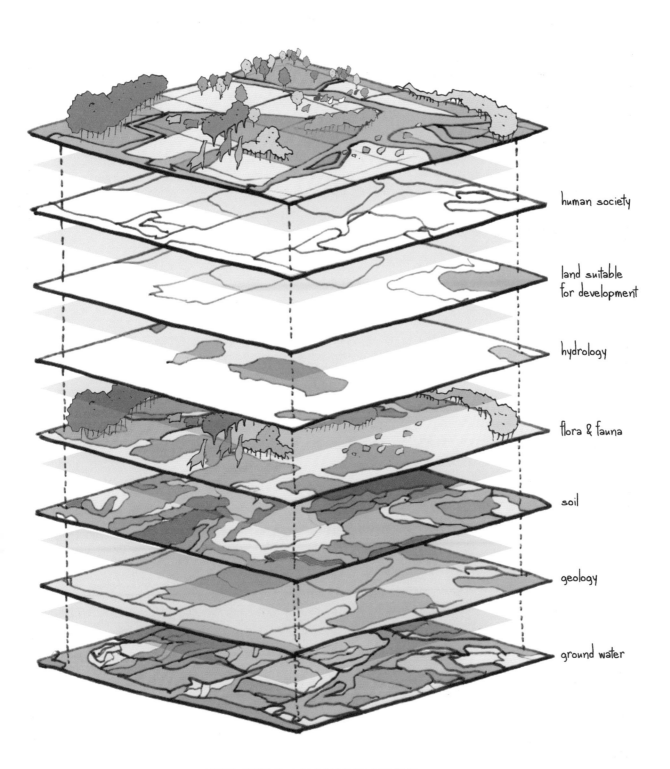

human society

land suitable
for development

hydrology

flora & fauna

soil

geology

ground water

ECOLOGICAL LANDUSE PLANNING

The crucial question for me then was how to advance this sophisticated ecology-based masterplanning method to the designing of an ecological architecture? I found the answer to bridging this gap was to use McHarg's ideas on ecological land-use and landscape planning to connect architecture with landscape constituents by creating a more organic architecture.

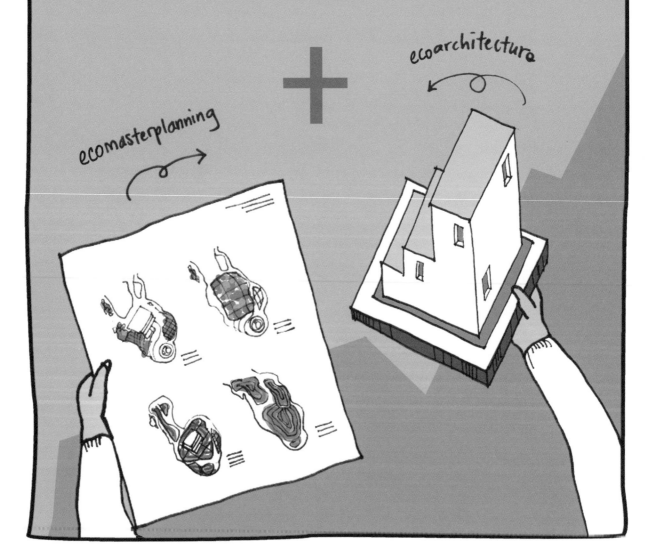

ecomasterplanning

+

ecoarchitecture

I started to look at the physical areal patterns for relating landscape elements to the essentially inorganic built environment. By studying system ecology in the work of <u>Odum (E.P.)</u>, of <u>Hollings (C.S.)</u>, and other ecologists it became clear that the biological structure of our existing built environment was incomplete.

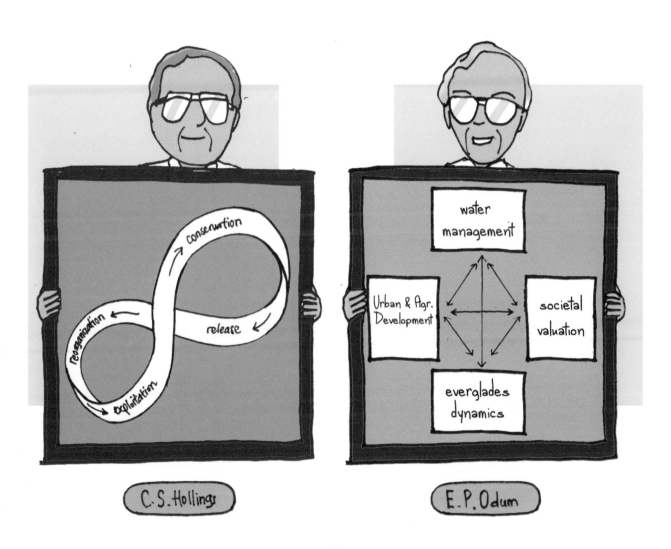

I concluded that architecture was almost entirely denatured- essentially **inorganic**- whereas, nature has a biological structure that has both biotic and abiotic constituents acting together to form a whole. It became clear that the vital biotic constituents in the **ecosystem were missing** in our present built environment or in any event existent in only superficially minimal content and this incompleteness in our built systems' biological structure needed to be redressed. I concluded that with our extensive building worldwide, of concrete structures, hardscapes, massive highways, and impervious surfaces, humans were simply clearing nature and replacing it extensively with inert inorganic mass- in effect, just about turning our planet into an inorganic, un-natural environment. I began readdressing this by looking at the various areal patterns in the placement of biotic constituents in built forms- essentially as habitats in the built environment. This became, for me, the starting point for the physical and visceral biointegration working toward the designing of an ecoarchitecture. I later refer to this greening of built forms as creating GREEN INFRASTRUCTURE.

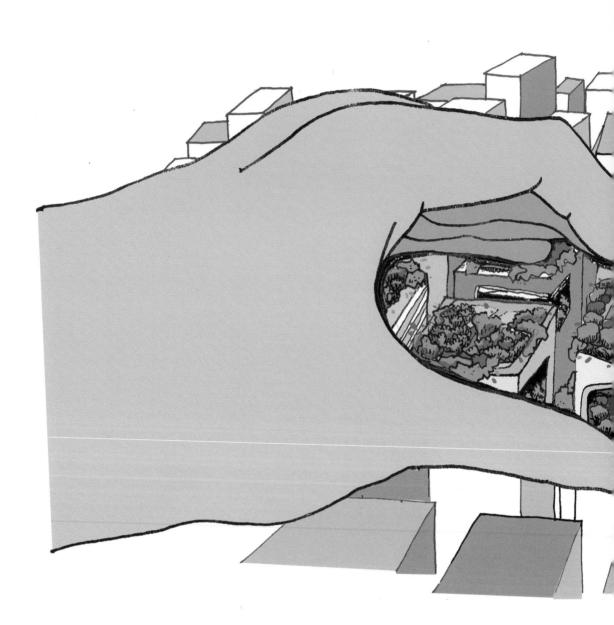

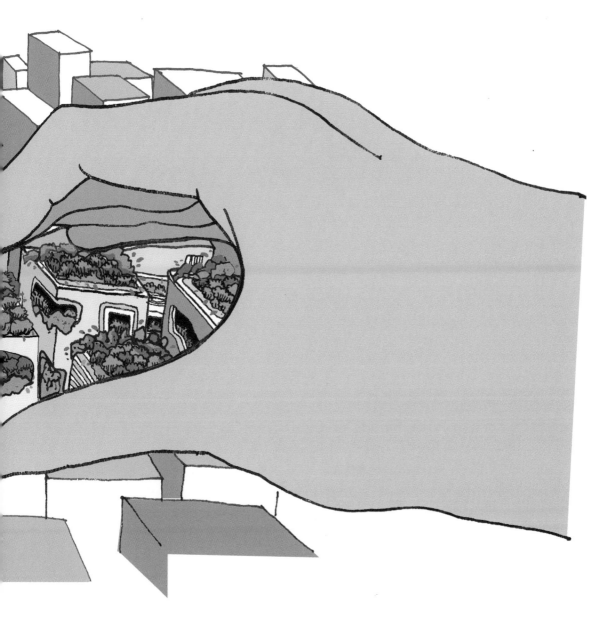

04 ECOLOGY AND SYSTEM
BIOINTEGRATION

I found that the ecologist sees the world differently, with an environmentally critical and holistic . They do not just consider the human world, but the natural and human-made world (as well as our human acts and activities) together, they examine the relations between the two – how one interacts and interfaces with the other. It became clear that our current state of environmental impairment is caused by design only with human society in mind, and not with the built environment in a way that functions in harmony with nature.

The crucial question I sought to answer in my work was how to achieve a **symbiotic biointegration** of our architecture, essentially our constructed environment (the artificial), with nature (the ecological) in design.

SYMBIOSIS

I concluded that the present conventional approach to design, whereby just addressing the built systems functional, aesthetic, and other aspects (i.e. location, behavior, etc.) to derive a well-tempered environmentally-serviced enclosure (Banham, R.), is inadequate.

CONTEXT

Now, taking nature into account, **we should no longer design a building simply as a synthetic structure disconnected from its natural surroundings.** We must now design with nature as a vital part, taking ecological context within the landscape into account. The designer must seek to achieve a seamless and benign relationship with nature's systems and the biospheric processes.

The recognition that all our built structures and their operations have interactions with and consequences on the environment's systems is crucial. This understanding needs to extend from the time we extract raw materials from the planet for our use to their treatment and manufacturing of materials and components of the built environment, to their transportation, to construction and operations over their lifetime, and, finally, to their eventual demolition, reuse, recycling, and seamless reintegration back into the natural environment at the end of their useful life.

START ● ● ● ● ● ● ● ● ● ● ● ● ● ● ● ● ▶ ● ● ● ● ● ● ● ● ● ● ● ● ● ● ● ● END

It is this **pervasiveness of human action** that differentiates us, as a species, from others in nature. It is when these acts are callously implemented upon the environment that there is a dislocation in the relationship between our built systems and the natural environment, and the consequences are detrimental.

Of course, not all our acts have negative impacts. Our built structures can be designed and constructed to inversely achieve positive net gains such as repairing, restoring, and regenerating previously fragmented natural landscapes to benefit ecosystem services. We can work toward this by creating a new ecological nexus, sequestering green house gasses emitted by our burning of fossil fuels for generating energy, enhancing local biodiversity by bringing back native species to devastated landscapes, conserving and eliminating the use of non-renewable resources, creating healthy local microclimates by revegetation, and by enabling beneficial biophilic effects of the natural environment on humans to enhance well-being. Ecodesign is not just an act of designing to have minimal or zero negative consequences, but can also be design to achieve net positive outcomes.

The ecologist regards homo sapiens as just one specie out of the thousands of species in nature, albeit, different from others because of the immense power they wield over nature.

Humans are, far more than any other species, able to radically modify the physical and biological realms of the planet, shaping massive changes to the landscape, altering waterways, and contaminating the aerial environment leading to global climate change.

We are able to move huge volumes of materials and goods to distant locations, to industrialize the mass production of materials and food, to build large clusters of human communities as urban developments and cities with huge, mega structures and super-tall buildings, and to make small, miniscule, and nano artifacts and machinery. Humans make more artifacts than any other species and the more we make, the more we clutter the planet with used, discarded, and unused products and materials. In the process, we also emit waste solids, liquids, and gases into the biosphere.

HUMANITY.

It is this immense power that humans have over nature that needs to be exercised responsibly, with great care and prudence. Ecologists regard our planet as a "closed system", and, being the only planet we know of that can sustain human life, we need to use our immense power over nature not as an exploiter of its resources but as its conserver and benevolent guardian.

63

Of course, at the same time we need to be aware that green criteria is not the only factor in design. It is just one of a multitude of crucial societal and functional factors that we need to address such as designing to enable a collective, basic quality of life and sense of well-being, designing for livability, and designing to fulfill factors of happiness.

Generally stated, there are a multitude of societal issues to be addressed such as abject poverty, inadequate shelter and sanitation, human trafficking, high unemployment, prevalent urban crime, etc., but surely all these become considerably easier to address if we have clean air, clean land, and clean water.

While my early work explored physical integration in the placement of landscaping and biotic constituents in built forms to emulate the biological structure of ecosystems, I concluded that it was not adequate. I needed to progress from physical integration to systemic biointegration.

I looked at the properties of organisms and living systems in the work of the Cambridge mathematician and philosopher, Alfred North Whitehead, a contemporary of Betrand Russell, in the "philosophy of the organism." I studied the generic properties of living systems and organisms in the General Systems Theory, developed by Ludwig Von Bertallanfy and others. And I found a corollary, albeit a tenuous one, between designing with nature and the work of Japanese Metabolist architects in the '60s such as Kisho Kurokawa and Arata Isozaki, whose work I had written about earlier at the AA. I also found an affinity in the work of Paolo Soleiri in his Arcosanti, and in the organic architectural ideas of Frank Lloyd Wright and Frei Otto. Our built systems must become "living systems," integral with nature. They must have all the compatible properties of ecosystems, and not be dead, inert, or contaminating.

I started by defining our ideal, sustainable, future built environment. What is our **ecotopia**? What are its conditions? How can we, in retrospect, apply these conditions to our present to ascertain what present action we need to take toward a desired future?

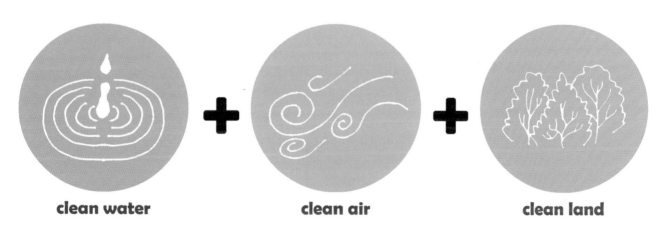

clean water   **clean air**   **clean land**

Clearly, the desired future has to be a sustainable one where our human habitats— our built environment— exist harmoniously, symbiotically, and mutually interdependent with nature— not contaminating, polluting, or simplifying it. To achieve this, our built environment cannot be estranged and isolated from nature as it is now. It must become **vitally linked to nature** in an ecological nexus and as an integral part of nature. The approach is to design with nature and not against it.

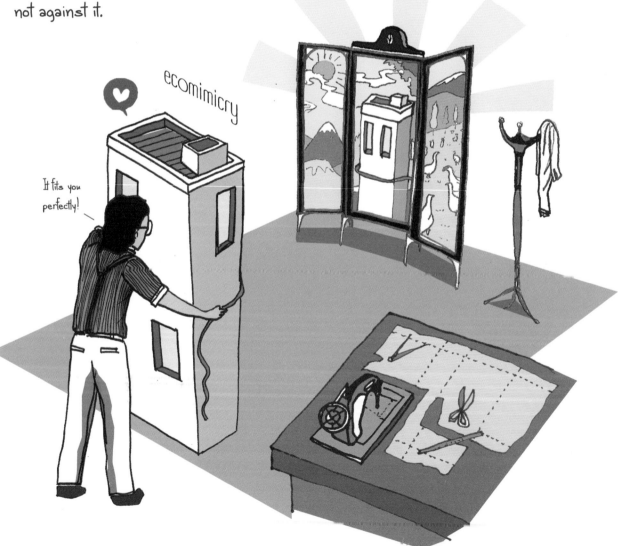

ecomimicry

It fits you perfectly!

68

To achieve a **stasis** with nature, our built environment must be like the natural systems in nature. To become like natural systems, built habitats must be analogous and a mimicry of natural ecological systems. The approach is not "biomimicry" (as in "bionics" and "biomechanics") but E C O M I M I C R Y in the emulation of the attributes of ecosystems. In seeking to emulating the attributes, properties, and processes of ecological systems, we can define the **ecosystem**

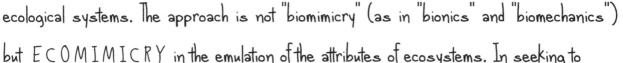

as a community of living organisms in conjunction with the non-living components of their environment

(i.e., air, water, and mineral soil), interacting holistically as a system.

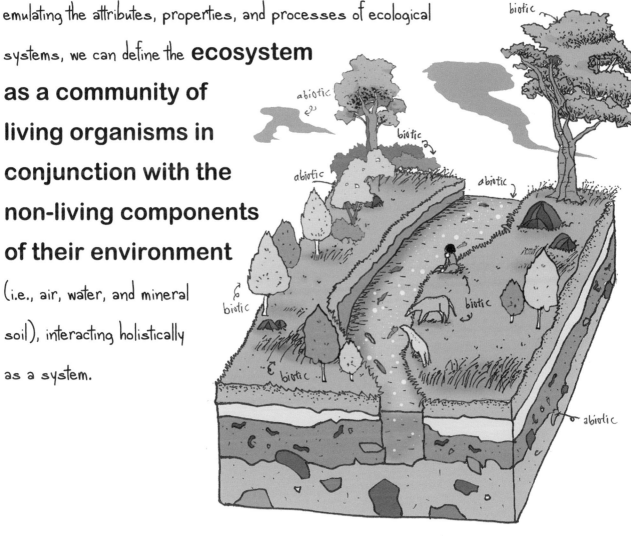

This concept provides the fundamental basis for all of our work on ecological architecture, where our designed systems become, in effect, "constructed ecosystems" that function integrally with nature. They should not be isolated, denatured, or physically divorced from the natural environment.

The fundamental premise is that ecological systems had existed in nature as sustainable systems long before humans became prominent exploiters of nature. These have always been in a general state of stasis, self-supporting, self-sustaining, and interdependent. While this state of stasis does not always exist in ecosystems, an analogic and emulating approach ensures greater likelihood for long-term survivability.

I sought to create a human built environment that emulates the attributes,

functions, structure, and processes of ECOSYSTEMS as a

"constructed ecosystem" - as a built system

functioning as a living system within nature.

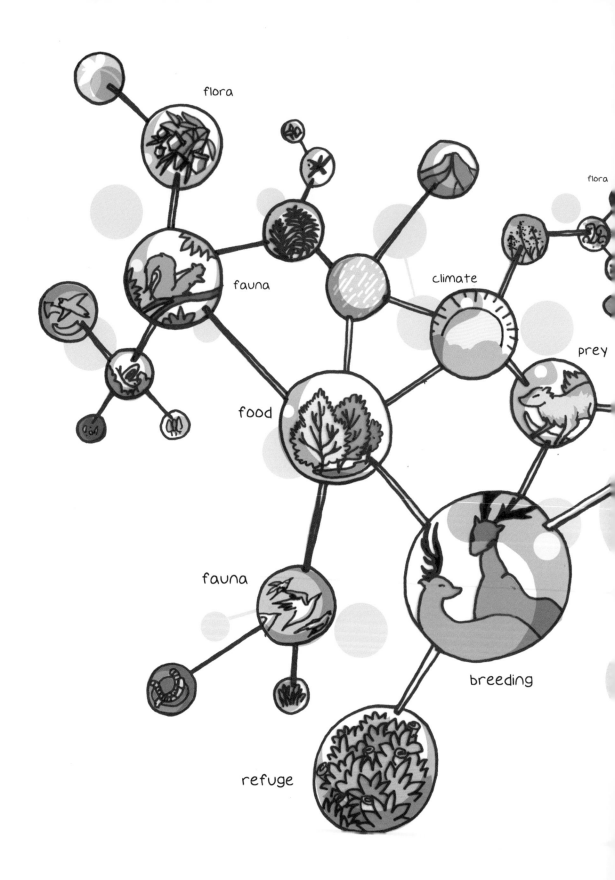

flora

fauna

climate

flora

prey

food

fauna

breeding

refuge

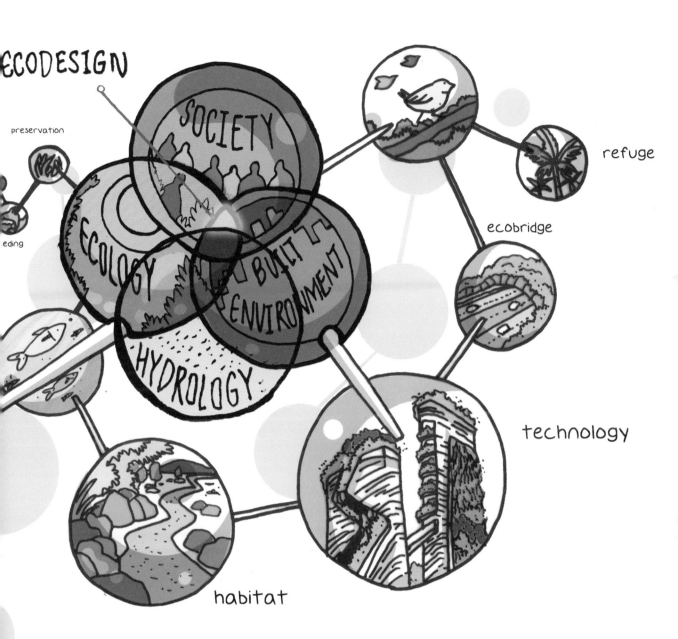

ECODESIGN

preservation

eding

SOCIETY

ECOLOGY

BUILT ENVIRONMENT

HYDROLOGY

refuge

ecobridge

technology

habitat

05 BIOLOGICAL STRUCTURE OF ECOSYSTEMS

Ecosystems are not static systems but go through stages of succession. In emulating the attributes of ecosystems, particularly at its late stages of succession, we find that the ecosystem's physical-biological structure has a complement of both ORGANIC constituents (biotic) as well as INORGANIC constituents (abiotic) that act together to form a whole. Whereas

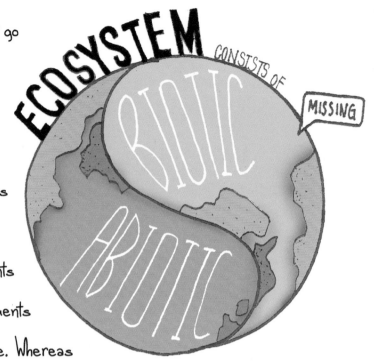

if we look at the biological structure of our existent human built environment, it is evident that it is essentially inorganic. It is devoid of any significant biotic content. For our built environments to be constructed ecosystems,

they must have a similar complement of both biotic and abiotic constituents that function holistically. The next step in creating an ecoarchitecture is to design built environments to have a complement of both biotic and abiotic constituents.

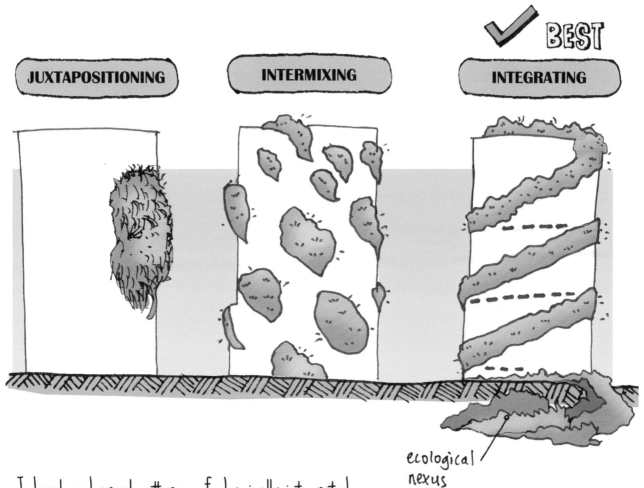

JUXTAPOSITIONING

INTERMIXING

✓ **BEST**

INTEGRATING

ecological nexus

I developed areal patterns of physically integrated,

inorganic constituents of our built systems with the organic landscape constituents.

This intertwining and continuous pattern is

ecologically preferred in order to share natural

resources, which engenders a higher probability of biodiversity and enables greater

species interaction and movement.

Many of the architects who imitate my work just place vertical landscaping in their buildings, but my contention is that green architecture has to be considerably more than just the physical placement of biotic constituents and vegetation in built forms.

I found that a step toward greater systemic biointegration of the biotic with the abiotic constituents in built forms occurs through designing built systems as a range of H A B I T A T S within the built forms and around its site, which must be connected to the surrounding landscape hinterland. Habitats are areas where particular groups of species live. The habitats could be within our built system, at the ground plane, green walls, in planted terraces and courtyards in built forms, in open atriums, or in enclosable spaces that are operable depending on the season of the year.

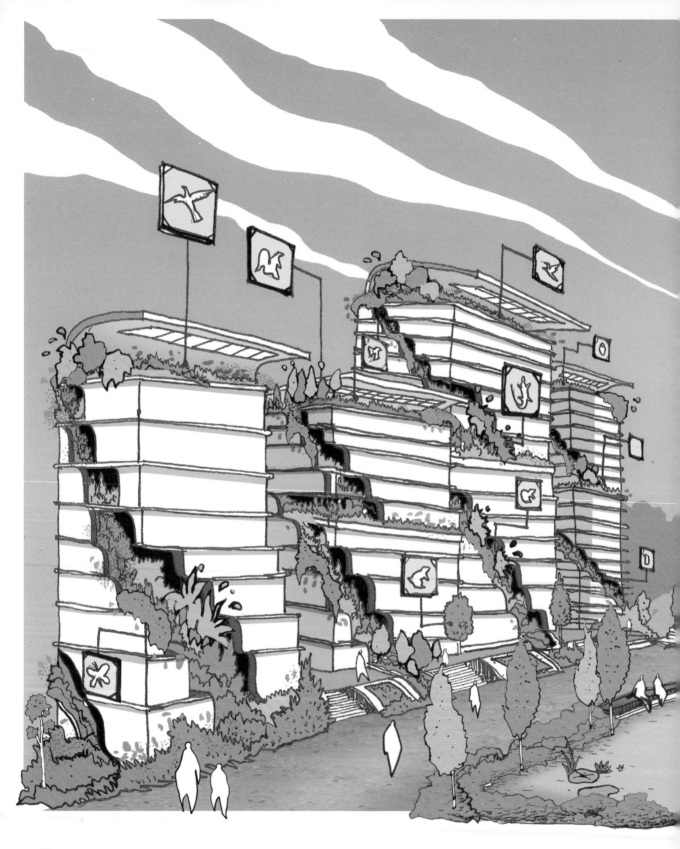

For each of the habitats in our built system, we need to identify the suitable native species of fauna to inhabit these that are not hazardous to humans in relation to their need for feeding, breeding, or refuge. We then need to include, in the habitats, the appropriate NATIVE SPECIES of flora that will attract these fauna. This is followed by the construction of the appropriate landscape conditions that will enable these species of flora and fauna to survive the seasons of the year. What we then have, in total, is a built structure that is a constructed ecosystem — that is a Living System in which physical constituents (the hardscape architectural parts) are integral with the natural constituents. The entire designed system is no longer an inert or "dead" artifact that is a denatured architectural structure.

This endeavor advances McHarg's work beyond ecological land-use planning to the realm of architectural design through systemic biointegration of otherwise inert synthetic building systems with local  and through the creation of habitats, which are connected in an ecological nexus with the natural ecology and hinterland such that, altogether, these become a continuous, connected green ecoinfrastructure. This contributes to reconnecting the fragmented landscape, enhancing the biodiversity of our built structures and their sites, and providing common ecosystem services.

This GREEN ECOINFRASTRUCTURE

(whether horizontal at the ground plane, or vertically climbing up the built form), once connected to the surrounding landscape and its hinterland becomes a part of the biome. **Our built environment is no longer an inert, artificial, and denatured item, estranged, isolated, and cauterized from the natural environment**. It is no longer destructive and parasitic on nature, but an integral part of nature that can serve restorative, reciprocal, and symbiotic ecosystem purposes.

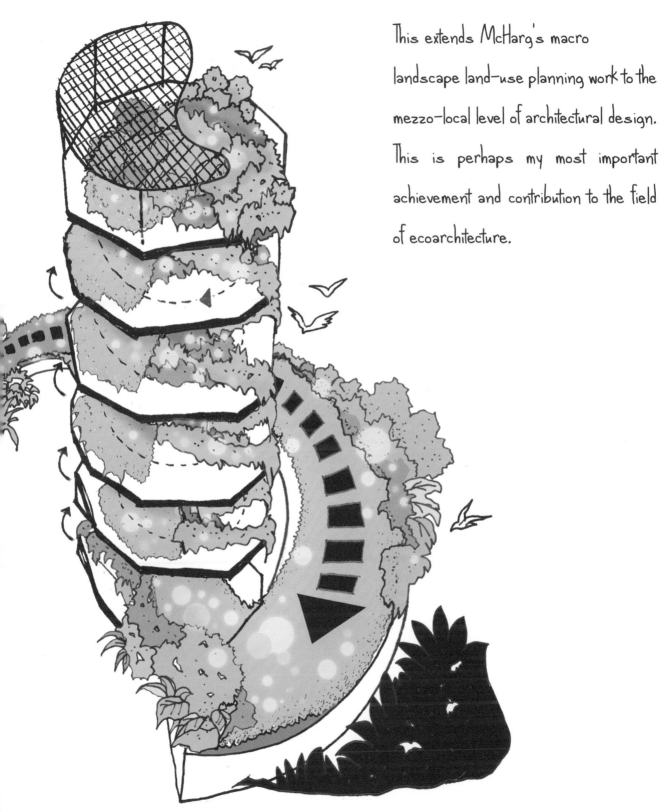

This extends McHarg's macro landscape land-use planning work to the mezzo-local level of architectural design. This is perhaps my most important achievement and contribution to the field of ecoarchitecture.

Besides emulating the biological structure of ecosystems, we need to emulate the other properties and functions of an ecosystem— especially in its later stages of succession in order to achieve an enhanced systemic relationship.

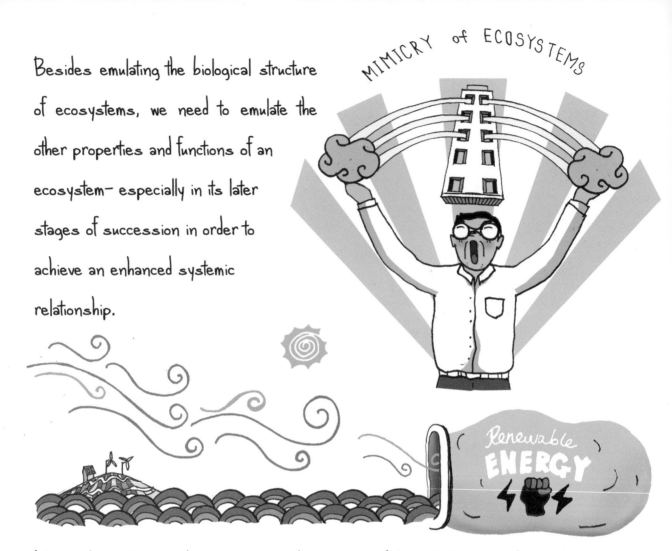

We need to achieve a biointegration in built systems' through the use of environmental and technological functions and processes that <u>mimic the other processes and functions of ecosystems</u>.

These include the use of energy from renewable sources in built systems, which need to be designed and constructed as <u>net zero energy structures</u> that are carbon neutral.

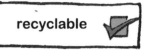
recyclable ✓

biodegradable ✓

reuseable ✓

carbon neutral ✓

We need to design the built environment's internal MATERIAL

PROCESSES in a cyclic use of resources: through reuse and recycling to the eventual

reintegration of biodegradable and non-biodegradable— no longer reusable— materials seam—

less back into the environment as zero waste.

We need to manage the hydrology as a net water system

to close the water cycle in our built systems and to regenerate

the ground water.

We need to carefully manage the assimilation and sequestering

of our built environment's gaseous and liquid emissions into

the environment to be within its carrying capacity, and without

contamination.

A UNIFIED THEORY for ecodesign

My Cambridge doctoral dissertation was focused on the theoretical aspects of ecological design and planning. I used a General Systems Theory model (from Ludwig von Bertallanfy), combined with the work on the systems theory of ecological systems (Odum, E. P. et. al.), to develop an abstract, theoretical model for ecodesign.

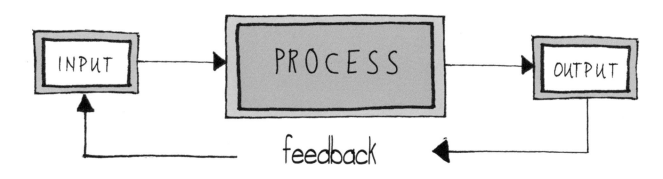

INPUT → PROCESS → OUTPUT

feedback

This is perhaps my other  contribution to this field. I formulated a unified, empirical, theoretical model for ecodesign in the form of a comprehensive framework as a "partitioned matrix," used by mathematicians to represent the key sets of interactions in ecodesign.

An obvious conclusion from the theoretical model is that achieving symbiosis in green design is a considerably more complex enterprise than it is perceived by many green designers. It is clear that green design is much more than just fulfilling conventional accreditation systems (such as LEED), and must concurrently address all the sets of interdependent interactions.

My doctoral dissertation was published in the late '70s by McGraw Hill. I entitled it **Design**ing **with Nature** as a tribute to McHarg's earlier benchmark book, *Design with Nature*. The book was later republished in Spanish by Gilli and Gilli.

With these first steps in place, I thought I was set to put my studies into practice in the real world, but it soon became evident that this earnest intention was more difficult than I had anticipated.

REALITY

RITIC

MONEY

06 DESIGNING IN THE
REAL WORLD

 Upon the completion of my doctoral dissertation I was considering what to do next? I had, in my final year at Cambridge, arranged for the Japanese Metabolist architect Kisho Kurokawa, to speak at the Department of Architecture as a visiting lecturer.

During his visit, and over a conversation, Kurokawa advised that upon the completion of my studies at Cambridge I should return to Malaysia to help in the building of the nation as an architect. I become a fully fledged professional architect upon passing my RIBA Part 3. I left Cambridge and went back to the real world in the Far East, starting with the firm Arkitek Bersekutu, based in Kuala Lumpur in 1974. I worked there for a year, mostly under the celebrated Malay architect,

khabar baik!

. I left within a year to join my fellow alumni from the AA, Tengku Robert Hamzah, a Prince from the Kelantan Malay Royal family, who had just started a private practice.

Hijjas Kasturi

Hi Tengku!

It was the mid '70s, and it had been five years since I had completed my student internship in Singapore. I quickly discovered that architectural school did not prepare me (or any student) for professional practice. I now had to face the world of the building industry as a commercial architect in practice. This was a new environment: dealing with clients and staff issues; negotiating and collection of fees; planning cash flows; designing and delivering on time and within budget; and the supervision of construction work to ensure a high quality outcome.

REALITY

Malaysia is not exactly a third-world country, but neither is it a first-world. To me, it was a $2\frac{1}{2}$ world— a resource rich, rapidly developing country. This world of business was a new way of life to me, and an environment that is entirely different from academia. I was partially prepared for this after my earlier internship in Singapore, which helped me make the transition less jarring.

It became evident that it was extremely difficult to apply the theoretical work from my Cambridge dissertation to the regime of design in a professional architectural practice – the theoretical work was simply too abstract. Furthermore, the practice of ecodesign was still very much in its infancy in the mid '70s. It was not the priority of the day in a rapidly developing environment where the priorities were achieving the lowest cost in the fastest time. Green design was outside the realm of what the conventional, local, private, and public sectors clientele wanted. Not being topical, I received no support from my fellow professional engineering consultants who seemed non-existent.

Seeking to do ecoarchitecture and ecoengineering was way off-tangent from the professional engineers' beaten track. It was not until the '90s that I finally got some early engineering support, starting with the UK firm of Battle McCarthy (Guy Battle & Chris McCarthy).

Upon entering the commercial world, I found that I needed now a total change in mindset from an academic one to one that addresses the cut-and-thrust world of business. Without a clue of how to conduct business as a professional architect, I had to quickly learn the rudiments of business and acquire business acumen in a sink-or-sink situation.

My cousin Gary, a businessman, advised me of the necessity of attending classes at a local management school. So I went to the Malaysian Institute of Management and attended all the available evening classes in business administration and management on <u>leadership, marketing, organization, delegation, and finance</u>. The knowledge from these classes gave me the crucial springboard needed to catch up to, and compete with, the existing large architectural firms that have been around for some time.

Formal schooling in business gives one a sharper and more confident edge when competing with existing, large architect firms. The principals of these firms, having been around for many years, acquired their business acumen and "T R I C K O R T R A D E" intuitively and through trial-and-error. With proper schooling, I acquired the business acumen for professional practice rapidly, and, more importantly, systematically. The orderly acquisition enabled a swifter and more confident approach to addressing business problems and development problems, and commercial issues, opposed to the hit-or-miss intuitive solutions of the unschooled.

I also received advice on architectural discourse from Roy Landau, the head of the AA's Graduate School at the time. But as a designer, I still had to find a way of designing that was palatable to the local clientele, but, that also had bearing to my doctoral dissertation and ecological agenda. This was the next issue that I had to address.

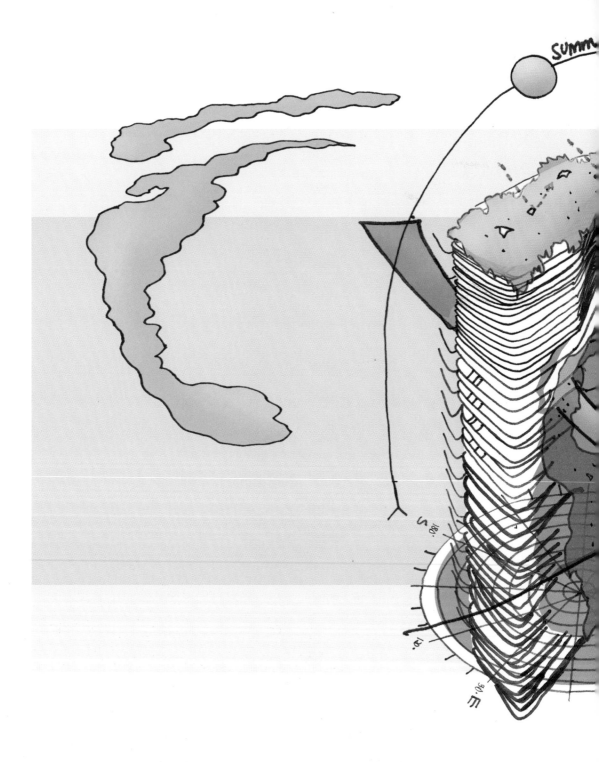

WINTER

07 BIOCLIMATIC
DESIGN

I found the answer in ⟨ **BI✿CLIMATIC DESIGN** ⟩. This directive came from a conversation with Alvin Boyarsky, the then Chairman of the AA School. After our meeting I started to research design with the climate in the work of the Olgyay's (Victor and Alidar), Giovoni (Baruch), and Koenigsberger (Otto). Koenigsberger was, for a short time, the head of the Tropical School of Architecture at the AA during the early '60s, which my business partner, Tengku Robert Hamzah attended. I later befriended Olgyay Jr. (Olgyay Senior's son) who I later wrote a forward for in the 2015 republication of his father's milestone book, *Design with Climate*.

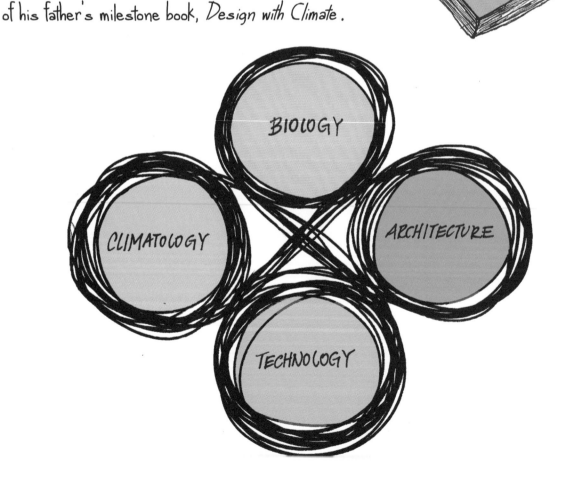

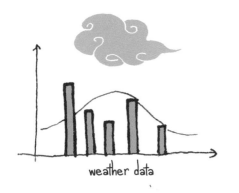

weather data

INFLUENCE

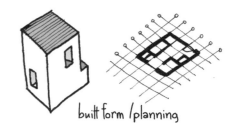

built form /planning

BI🌱CLIMATIC DESIGN is the designing of built forms and planning layouts, taking the seasonal meteorological data and climate of the built form's locality into account. I soon found that this design approach provided the ideal starting point as an armature for ecodesign. Bioclimatic design is often also referred to as **PASSIVE MODE DESIGN** as it results in a built form that is passively low-energy in its performance, enabling enhanced internal comfort conditions over the external conditions without the inclusion of any active environmental engineering systems.

Roof-Roof House (1986)

101

I regard **BIOCLIMATIC DESIGN** as a <u>subset</u> of ecological design. The basic premise is that if our built forms starts out designed as passive ↓ENERGY, the optimization of all of its passive bioclimatic design responses (appropriate configuration with consideration to the local <u>sun path</u>, responsive <u>facade design</u>,

Ecological Design

bioclimatic design

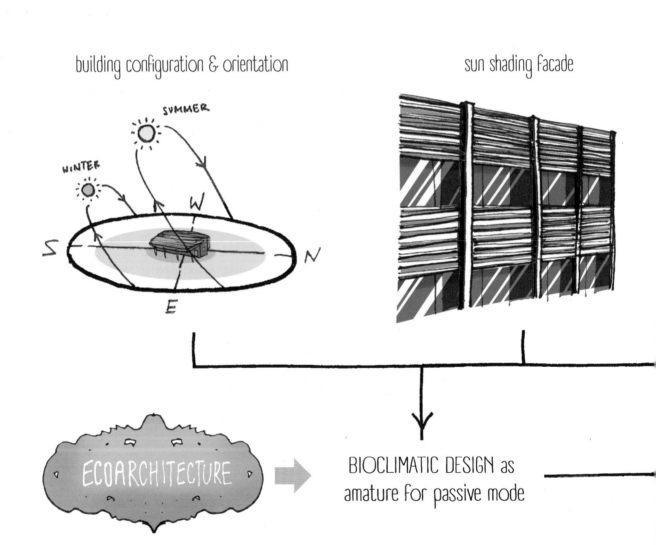

building configuration & orientation

SUMMER

WINTER

W

S

N

E

sun shading facade

ECOARCHITECTURE ➡ BIOCLIMATIC DESIGN as amature for passive mode the appropriate use of <u>building mass</u>, the use of <u>passive devices</u> to optimize the ambient energies of a place, by site layout, etc.) then becomes a framework for the subsequent inclusion of active, clean tech, environmental ecoengineering systems. Bioclimatic design enhances internal comfort conditions for its users and enables further enhancements of their low energy building performance while addressing other ecological functions and features.

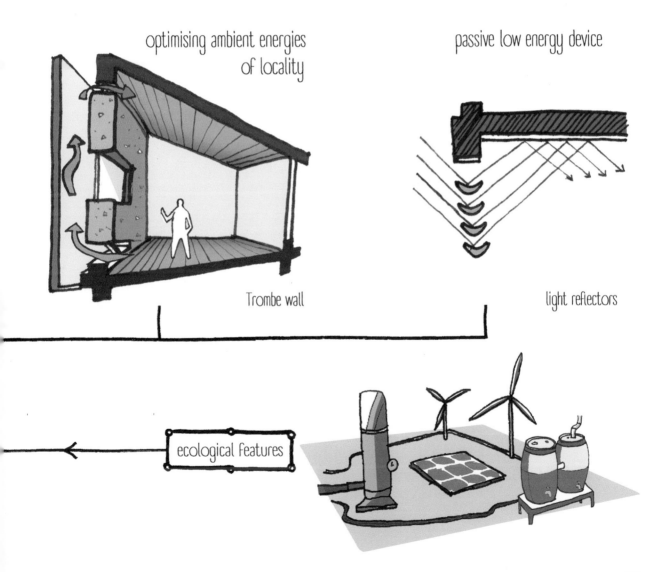

optimising ambient energies
of locality

passive low energy device

Trombe wall

light reflectors

ecological features

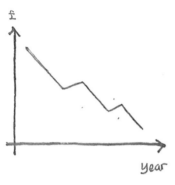

From around the mid '60s on, energy became relatively cheap and easily accessible. Schools of architecture stopped teaching students to relate their buildings to climate because cheap heating and air-conditioning was prevalent ...

... and they could design just about whatever iconic built forms they liked without considering their relationship with the climate of the place, which led to building of energy guzzling structures.

But, with the existing environmental decline today, <u>we cannot continue to ignore the influence of the natural environment and continue to design and build callously</u>, with negligence toward nature and non-renewable energy resources. As I had concluded earlier at the Technical Research Division in Cambridge, before we dwell on the engineering and technological systems of green design, we must start by looking at the ecology and climatic conditions of the local, natural environment to provide the baseline and context for design. We need to see how these affect all human acts and activities. Schools need to teach designing with climate again.

LIKE AN

ARMATURE FOR ECODESIGN,

the bioclimatic approach became the vital first step in ecodesign as <u>it provides the basic framework for green design.</u> We need, of course, to be clear that bioclimatic design is not ecodesign nor is it a substitute or panacea for ecodesign.

" My adopting of the bioclimatic design approach <u>appealed to the commercially-minded investor/developer client</u> because passive features enables low-energy performance architecture that saves on upfront costs and on subsequent operational costs. "

An incidental outcome of bioclimatic design is that resulting architectural forms tend to have configuration characteristics of shape, orientation, layout, and facade that arise from their response to the climatic conditions of the place, giving them a critical link to a **local climate**.

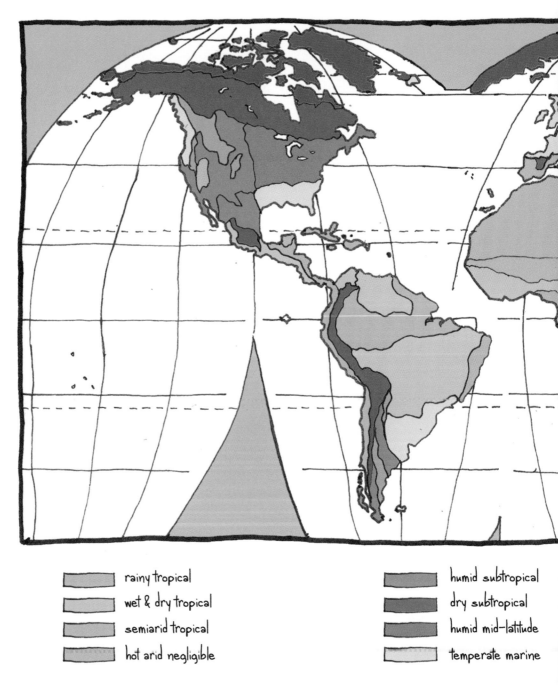

rainy tropical		humid subtropical
wet & dry tropical		dry subtropical
semiarid tropical		humid mid-latitude
hot arid negligible		temperate marine

This link, that may be unconsciously expressed in built form, will have an aesthetic quality that is based on the form-giving attributes of natural climatic forces. Frampton (K.) refers to this as "CRITICAL REGIONALISM".

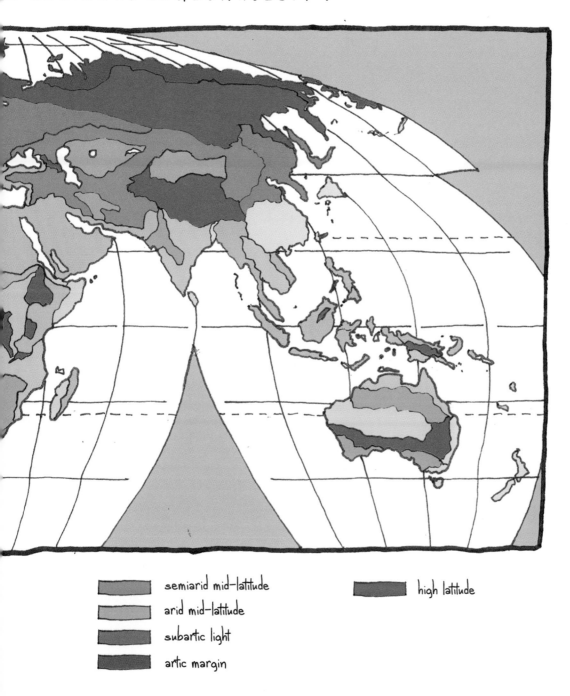

semiarid mid-latitude	high latitude
arid mid-latitude	
subartic light	
artic margin	

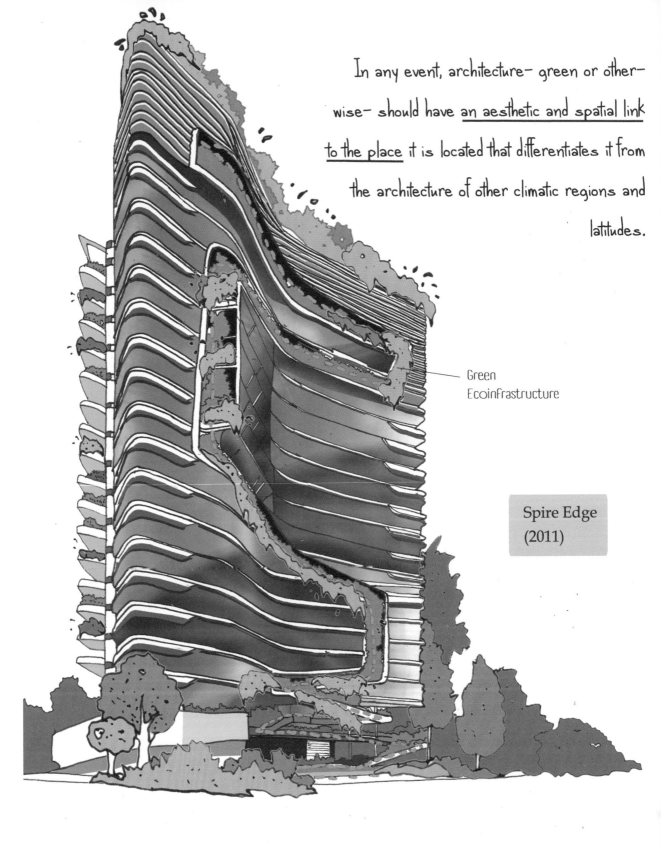

In any event, architecture- green or otherwise- should have an <u>aesthetic and spatial link to the place</u> it is located that differentiates it from the architecture of other climatic regions and latitudes.

Green
Ecoinfrastructure

Spire Edge
(2011)

But more than just this climatic link to the endemic aspects of the place, the architecture should also have a link with the **ecology of the place.**

biodiversity targets

habitat condition →	shrub roofs	grassland roofs	planted facades	densely wooded area	wet woodland

habitat condition ➡
- dominant plant species
- water quality
- water balance

indicator of biodiversity and primary associated spiecess

species	shrub roofs	grassland roofs	planted facades	densely wooded area	wet woodland
anthornis melanura	♥ ⬛ R	♥ ⬛ 🍗 R 💧	♥ ⬛ 🍗 R 💧	♥ ⬛ 🍗 R 💧	♥ ⬛ 🍗 R 💧
porphyrio hochstetteri		♥ ⬛ 🍗 R 💧	R	♥ ⬛ 🍗 R 💧	♥ ⬛ 🍗 R 💧
gallirallus australis		♥ ⬛ R 💧		♥ R	♥ ⬛ R 💧
zosterops lateralis	♥ ⬛ R	♥ ⬛ 🍗 R 💧	♥ ⬛ 🍗 R 💧	♥ ⬛ R 💧	🍗
australasian swamphen	R	♥ 🍗 R	♥ ⬛ 🍗 R 💧	🍗	♥ ⬛ 🍗 R 💧
mystacina tuberculata		♥ ⬛ R		♥ ⬛ R 💧	🍗
tadorna variegata		♥ 🍗 R 💧		R	♥ ⬛ 🍗 R 💧
heteralocha acutirostris	♥ ⬛ R	♥ ⬛ 🍗 R 💧	♥ ⬛ 🍗 R 💧	♥ ⬛ 🍗 R 💧	♥ ⬛ 🍗 R 💧

LEGEND

J F M A M J J A S O N D

season which they occur, if full means resident

🍗 feeding ♥ breeding ⬛ prey 💧 water R refuge

113

Experiencing an architecture that has a climate-responsive link enables users to become more aware of **where they are** — being in an architecture that is sensitive and responsive to its locational climatic features.

Putting in other features can further enable users to know **who they are** by being cognizant of the cultural factors of the locality. There is the need, at the same time, to avoid pastiche. The subsequent adoption of the prevalent technological systems of the day enables its users to become aware of **when they are** by reminding them that they are indeed in the 21st century and certainly not in the past.

This approach to design becomes very much a **"situationalist"** approach where the location of a built form takes on characteristics of the environment and sense of place. There is not a universal "One-solution fits all" design in international style that negates the specificity of place.

While some may contend that a design should place overt emphasis on the cultural context of its particular locality, I contend that a physical climatic link has greater significance because <u>climate is a more durable factor of place than time,</u> and other factors such as cultural or symbolism tend to be transient.

We can assert that designing with climate as a bioclimatic approach gives the architecture a more vital, differentiating, authentic, aesthetic identity.

My earlier studies of biological analogies led me understand my work as an ecodesigner as similar to the **work of doctors and surgeons** in the medical world of prosthesis design.

A **prosthesis** is an artificial, human-made device — usually synthetic — that is connected to its organic host. The organic host to a prosthesis is the human body. It can be a replacement of a damaged, missing, or cauterized part of its organic host, but if it is to function successfully it has to biointegrate seamlessly with its host organism as an appendage. The goal of prosthetic design is to provide solutions that enable effective biointegration of the artificial device with its organic host.

By analogy, our human built environment is similar to a prosthetic device because it is an entirely synthetic, human-made artifact connected to a host organism—equivalent to the human body in medical situation—which is the biosphere and the ecosystems in which our built environment must successfully, seamlessly, and benignly biointegrate. The failure of our existing built environment— our cities, industries, and utilities—to biointegrate seamlessly with the natural environment has caused the present environmental decline.

To redress this, we need to redesign and achieve better biointegration of our built environment with the biosphere. Of course, achieving this is easier said than done. This is the crucial challenge of ecodesign: to achieve an environmentally seamless biointegraton of our human-made,

built environment as a constructed ecosystem with the naturally occurring ecosystems in a reciprocal and <u>symbiotic relationship</u>...

... as opposed to one that is estranged, inert, and parasitic.

If a crucial objective is to achieve a successful biointegration, then our human society should be able to successfully biointegrate everything that it builds and makes, and will prioritize it in all acts relating to the natural environment in order to create in a seamless, benign, restorative, and mutually interdependent way — within nature's carrying capacity. If we can accomplish this we could eliminate environmental problems altogether. This is the key objective in ecodesign, but what does biointegration mean?

I regard this biointegration at three levels :

physical, systemic, and temporal.

foliage

contour

water

Physical biointegration is the integration of our designed systems with the physical characteristic of the place. Systematic biointegration is the integration of our designed system's functions a processes with the natural processes of the place. Temporal biointegration is the sustainable u: of natural resources in our designed systems so that they coincide with natural renewal and re plenishment rates and cycles.

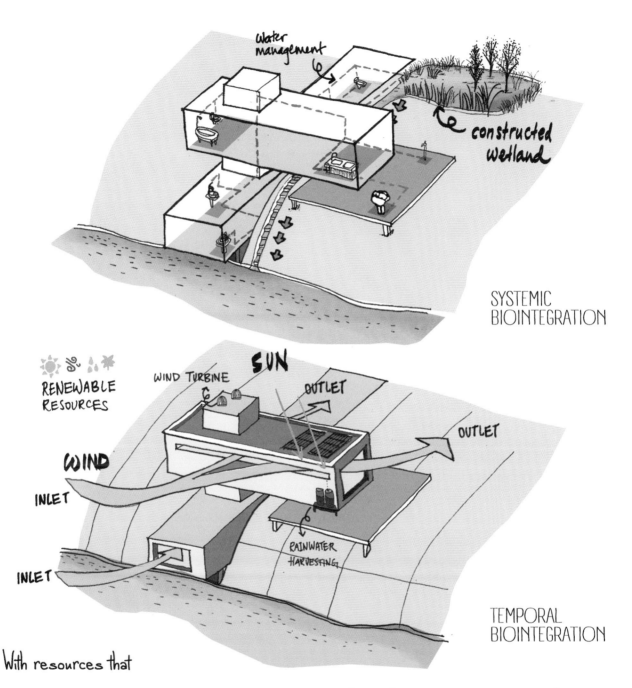

Water
management

constructed
wetland

SYSTEMIC
BIOINTEGRATION

RENEWABLE
RESOURCES

SUN

WIND TURBINE

OUTLET

OUTLET

WIND

INLET

RAINWATER
HARVESTING

INLET

TEMPORAL
BIOINTEGRATION

With resources that

have extensively long replenishment cycles such as fossil fuels, our approach must be one

of conservation, reducing the rate of consumption, and the replacement of their use with

renewable sources such with solar and wind energy.

10 MATERIAL AND ZERO WASTE

Humans extract materials and natural resources from the environment and use these to mass manufacture artifacts industrially. These material and components are combined for societal use in built structures, as instruments for work, lifestyle, and domestic use ; for recreational purposes such as toys , cameras, and electronics ; for mobility items such as cars, buses, trucks, trains, and aircrafts ; for production of household goods such as stoves, irons, and food products ; and for communication and mobile phones.

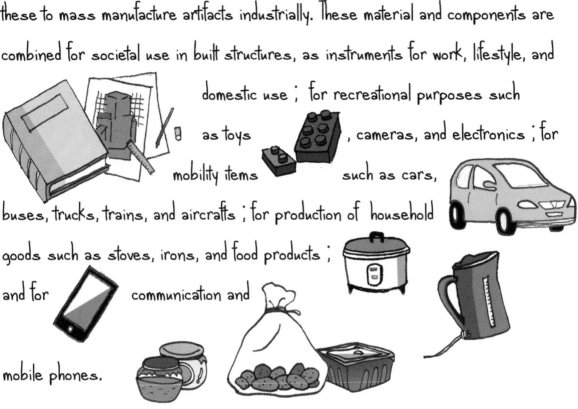

With the exception of some organic products made from natural materials, most manufactured items are not biodegradable. Some of these have fixed locations such as buildings, but others— vehicles, electronic products, etc.- have no fixed abode,. No nother species in nature is as profuse in the industrailised mass production of non-biodegradable artifacts as humans.

Humans make artifacts in excessive quantities, which has led to the critical issue of their disposal into the natural environment. Most of these items, after use, will end up in landfills or will be discarded into the natural environment, seas, and waterways, which affects the aquatic ecosystems and marine life as well.

We need to change the manner in which we use materials. Primarily, material use is a linear throughput system in which humans will use an artifact and then throw it away after use—a one-way flow—into a cyclic system. In ecological reality, there is no

AWAY because the planet is a closed system and these used artifacts become waste that ends up somewhere on the planet: whether on the ground as litter, as rubbish in landfills, in an accumulating scrapyard, or dumped into the waterways or seas.

We need to regard the use of materials in and for our built environment as part of the cyclic flow in the totality of the natural systems and processes. Reducing our depletion of those non-renewable material resources with long, natural replenishment cycles means conserving, and, where possible, extending their useful life through reuse and recycling within the built environment. In addition, <u>we need to seek ways to seamlessly reintegrate materials back into the natural environment</u> at the end of their useful life in order to facilitate their replenishment. This is problematic because much of the material humans use in its built environment is non-biodegradable. In the case of metallic materials, their reconstitution is an option (opposed to disposal in a landfill), but this, in most instances, requires further use of energy resources. Ideally the energy should be from **renewable sources**.

In emulating the attributes of ecosystems in biomimicry where our built systems are constructed ecosystems, **we need to mimick the way the natural ecosystem handles outputs within the ecosystem**

where the wastes from one organism are recycled to become the food for another organism, and where materials are recycled within the ecological system and are biodegradable.

To achieve zero waste, after biodegradable materials are used they <u>should be returned to the environment within their time scales for biodegredation.</u> Even for those materials that are organic and biodegradable, there may need to be some facilitation for their seamless reintegration back into the natural environment.

We need to re-use everything we make, or recycle. Even if the material is a downgraded form from use it needs to be reconstituted into the original form for remanufacture. For those materials and artifacts that are not easily biodegradable, or that cannot be reused or recycled, we need to find ways to address what we do with these before seeking to **reconstitute them back into raw materials**, incurring extensive energy use. For the non-biodegradable material, we need to disassemble and retain these for reuse as much as possible within our built environment, until they have no further reuse potential within the built environment.

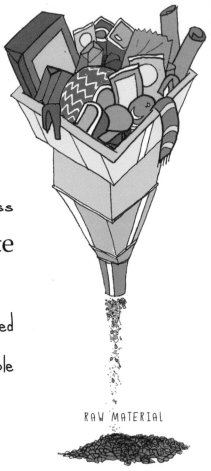

RAW MATERIAL

As mentioned earlier, buildings and those artifacts that are non-biodegradable, or that have long biodegradation periods, should have a projected trajectory for the end of their life cycle **designed into them** so that what happens at the end of their useful life, and where they will go, is already planned. We need to consider how the material at the end of this flow can be addressed.

We need to design with the outset of the product or artifact's afterlife in mind prior to their production. The latter is crucial as we need to eliminate the question of their disposal inasmuch as possible throughout their entire life-cycle. This also requires a society-wide management system at a scale that matches the industrial scale of its production to affect their return, their reuse, and recycling.

In the selection of materials for our built system we have to consider the extent of energy (especially non-renewable energy) that is consumed to produce, recycle, and dispose of the non-biodegradable products and materials in order to reintegrate them with the natural environment.

I contend that students of architecture should learn about materials more profoundly — not just how and whether materials are assembled, but the environmental consequences of the use of a material from source to site, to design for disassembly, and for reuse and recycling with the objective of achieving net waste. Hence, our attitude toward material use and selection becomes a very different approach to what is conventional. The knowledge needed for ecodesign today is considerably more complex than it ever has been.

A reduction in the production of materials and artifacts and a reduction in their consumption in excess of the basic needs of society will result in the reduction of extraction and use of these natural resources, a reduction in use of non-renewable energy resources, and a reduction in the negative consequences to the environment like the emission of green house gasses, and solid and liquid waste discharged into the natural environment.

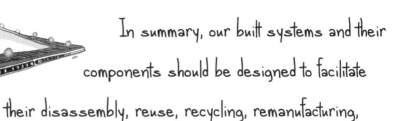

In summary, our built systems and their components should be designed to facilitate their disassembly, reuse, recycling, remanufacturing, reconstitution, and reintegration back into the environment prior to assembly. We can refer to this approach as "DFDRR" or **Designing for Disassembly, Reuse and Recycling**.

To facilitate this, we can design this into the building material by dimensional, modular standardization of components that can be easily disassembled, reused, and reassembled elsewhere.

11 EXISTING CITIES&BUILDING

Besides designing built forms, an ecodesigner needs to look at the greater context of where our designed systems are placed to find out what we could do to rectify the damage that humans have insensitively inflicted on the ecosystems. Examples of such callous acts include deforestation, the flattening of hills and landscapes through extensive earthworks, bisecting them with structures (roads and highways, drains, buildings, fencing, railway lines), and paving areas with impervious surfaces that seal the ground beneath.

Humans have essentially chopped up nature.

sea pollution   deforestation   disconnection   air pollution   exploitation   contaminatio

In restoring the landscape that has been fragmented by humans, we need to reconnect existing habitats with a new ecological nexus in order to create continuous green areas and biomes in/with existing structures that are not separate from a site or the hinterland. This reconnection, MAKING NATURE WHOLE , in an ecological nexus is a horizontal act across the landscape and vertical in built forms. This nexus is a form of green ecoinfrastructure that restores water balance, enables greater species interaction and migration, and creates a larger pool of natural resources available for sharing between species— leading to more biodiversity and a greater potential for survival without human support and ecosystem restoration.

link to hinterland

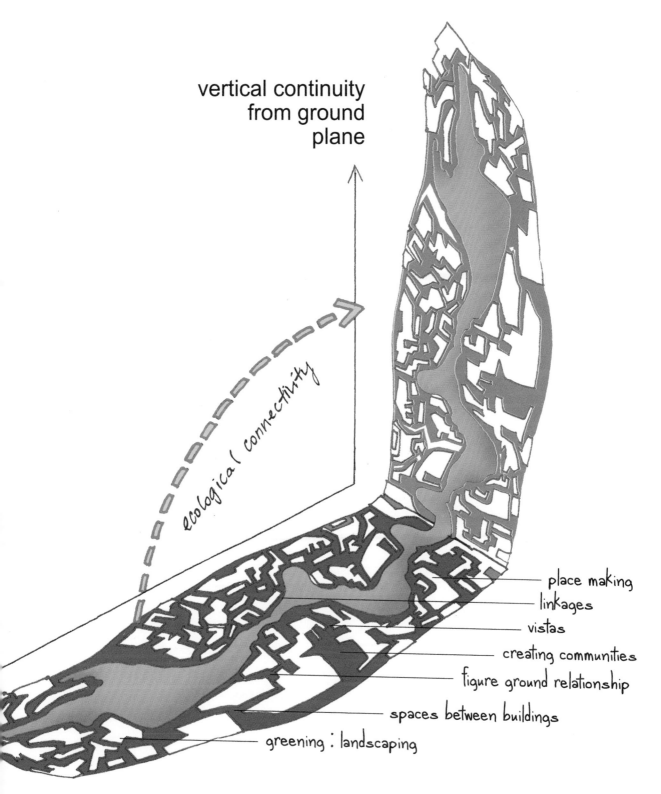

vertical continuity
from ground
plane

ecological connectivity

place making
linkages
vistas
creating communities
figure ground relationship
spaces between buildings
greening : landscaping

We can use constructed devices to RE-LINK N A T U R E in devastated landscapes with fragmented urbanscapes through the use of eco-bridges, eco-undercrofts, and eco-tunnels. Green ecoinfrastructure is "Nature's utilities," and crucial to the provision of common ecosystem services.

Ecobridge

More important than designing green developments and buildings is the greening of our existing cities. Many existing buildings have not been ecologically designed, and, since they outnumber new buildings, the retrofitting of existing buildings (and our cities) to make them ecologically resilient is more urgent than designing new green buildings.

While the increasing number of built green buildings contributes to our sustainable future, developing ecoarchitecture is only one aspect of sustainable design. Achieving environmental benefits is more than just creating individual green buildings or large clusters of green buildings; the macro approach should be the entire city and its various infrastructural systems that need to be greened. This is likely where the fight to save the environment in our cities will be won or lost.

In the re-planning and restoration of our built environments and cities into ecocities the obvious starting point is the engineering — the transportation systems that need to be reinvented, the utilities that need to be made into or replaced with green systems, and the use of smart IT systems.

One of the key steps is to start connecting the existing green areas within the city: green belts, parks, roadside margins, hedges, green roofs, green walls, and the landscape design such that all become invaluable habitats for enhancing biodiversity. These areas were originally green fields that were previously contiguous but have now been fragmented by human actions. These should now be reconnected to form new, linked green ecoinfrastructure regions as a new network of connected green areas.

I see this as the first, if not the key, step in any endeavor to making any existing city into an **ECOCITY** that reconnects——as much as possible——green areas and natural systems in order to create a biodiverse habitat to bring ecosystem services back to the city. This engenders the enhancement of health and sustainability of the city's natural systems and its surroundings, encourages the return of native species, enhances the previously obliterated biodiversity, and aids in the rehabilitation of degraded and partitioned landscapes.

Design, as a service industry, has limited power in society compared to a politically directed approach, which could target the city's businesses, transportation systems, infrastructure, recreation, and urban lifestyle to become green — not piecemeal, but in totality, simultaneously, and as rapidly as possible.

In looking at the flow of energy in ecosystems we find that ecosystems generally head toward **increased internal efficiency in energy use**, which is received from the sun through photosynthesis.

In ecomimicry, we need to design our constructed ecosystems (our built environments) to be increasingly efficient users of energy, and to use renewable sources of energy. The approach to designing for net zero energy built environments is a design process that starts with :

Firstly our optimization of all the **PASSIVE-MODE** (bioclimatic) design options to start out as a low-energy, passive-mode structures...

... followed by optimizing all the **MIXED-MODE** options, proceeding to the adoption of full, active-mode systems that must be the most efficient cleantech systems possible...

... and finishing with **PRODUCTIVE-MODE** systems in which the designed system produces its own energy from renewable sources.

12 LOOSE FIT
GREEN DESIGN

As mentioned earlier, designing is an anticipatory act. The designer must anticipate the trajectory of what will take place in his design (as well as its afterlife) before the designed system is built. The designer determines what would be the likely patterns and mode of use, user lifestyle, or work patterns within the designed system, and then designs the appropriate amount of space and volume, the configuration of enclosure, and environmental engineering systems for the level of expected comfort. There will be a need to "over-design" to allow for future flexibility in the event of permissible, unpredictable circumstances.

In effect, the designer determines the extent of F I T of the designed system with the design brief.

If the fit is too loose there will be wastage. If the fit is too tight or precise there will be no room for flexibility and future changes resulting in early demolition due to inadaptability to circumstances— a waste of the entire built structure. If the design is a LOOSE FIT structure, although having some built-in wastage (in materials, environmental systems, and other aspects), the "built-in redundancy" in the structure enables greater flexibility to change in future, and enables a structure to be recycled— increasing its useful life and leading to less wastage of the entire built form.

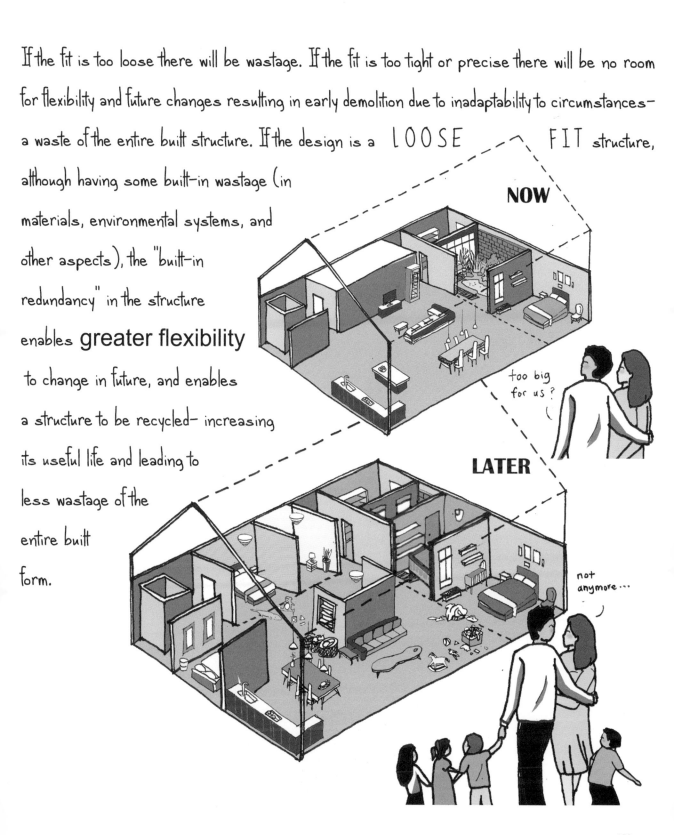

NOW

too big for us?

LATER

not anymore...

" One of my preoccupations is with the **aesthetics of green architecture** : what should a green building or assembly of buildings look like? We need to consider the aesthetics of our designs regardless of whether it is a building, artifact, or a masterplan. If a green building does not express itself as green, it confuses the layperson. "

An architect friend of mine once took an investor and me around a city center in North America.

This building is a green building and is accredited green...

Oh?

What do you mean by green?... It looks like any other building on this street..

Yea, but it has LEED Platinum certification..

It still looks like any other building on the street.

What this means is an aesthetic differentiation of green and non-green buildings is important.

I believe that any green building that we design, besides performing green, must be

AESTHETICALLY green and fulfilling.

Otherwise, we could have an instance where our buildings and artifacts may be 100 percent ecologically functional, but look PRISON LIKE, ungreen and have regimented inhumane internal spaces and nothing else.

In the '70s, one of the reasons why solar architecture failed was because it looked ugly, like built "plumbing" (after Scully, Vincent).

I do not think there is only one way to design, nor is there one singular green aesthetic. Different architects will have different ways of designing green architecture with different aesthetics.

If a green building should respond to its location's climate (bioclimatically) first, and then to **its ecology**, the outcome could likely look totally different from the conventional buildings of today. The biointegration of green matter and landscaping in a built form contributes to it looking alive with a "fuzzy," indeterminate hirsute aesthetic arising from its organic mass (vegetation).

While the aesthetic of the green built form is important, we need to ensure the iconic aesthetic features are **<u>not excessive</u>**. Overly gratuitous aesthetic features become wasteful, whereupon the built form becomes excessive in materials, resources, and technological systems.

13 BUSINESS OF ARCHITECTURE

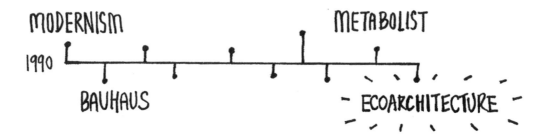

MODERNISM

1990

BAUHAUS

METABOLIST

ECOARCHITECTURE

I believe ecoarchitecture will be recorded in architectural history as a movement, as was Modernism a century ago. Already, a large segment of society realizes that green architecture is the way to design and build for our future. A dread is that before it gets embraced by all, a disaster——like a major, sudden, violent climate change——will result in tragedies to our human built environment that will force an ecologically-conscious design and way of life upon our society.

However, it is likely that green design will be just a "blip" in architectural history. Today, just about every architect claims to practice green design — some to a greater extent of authenticity and commitment than others. Within the near future it is likely that all architects will practice green design to a consistently high level of ecological authenticity and green design will become second nature in their design process.

Once this is prevalent, architects can then focus on doing what they should be doing all along, designing buildings and places that are immensely livable that will give pleasure and happiness to the people who use them. This is, after all, <u>the ultimate raison d'etre of architecture.</u> Achieving this is the incredible power that architecture and planning can have and could give to human society. I believe that there is more to being green than just designing and delivering green buildings.

While delivering ecological buildings contributes to our sustainable future, we need to be aware that this is only one aspect of the bigger picture as we move toward a resilient future. Many designers simplistically think that if we just design green buildings then all will be well for our sustainable future. This is simply not enough. Besides delivering green constructions, we concurrently need green businesses, green food production, green recreation, green mobility, green industries, green economics, green _____. We have to extend our endeavors as green designers to our clients. Our role is also to convince our clients to not only desire green buildings, but to make their own businesses, industries, and lifestyles green.

If we want our ecostructures (architecture and ecostructures) to be acceptable to society, we need to make these aesthetically satisfying and fulfilling. My contention is that a green architecture deserves its own aesthetic and a green building should look green and not like any other built forms. As a constructed ecosystem, its ecological systems can be aesthetically expressed.

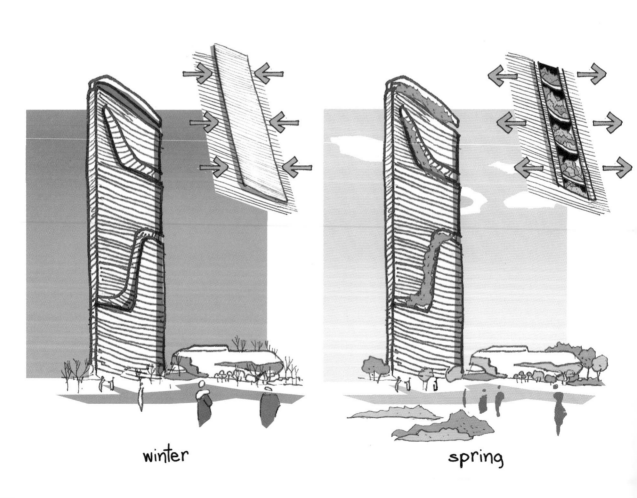

winter   spring

It should look like a **LIVING SYSTEM** (a reciprocal and symbiotic part of nature) and not like a non-living object, estranged from nature. A design proposition that remains to be developed for the future is S M A R T ecologically-responsive architecture — a city that automatically changes its facade, form, and function with the changing external environment, seasons of the year, and ecological changes in the nature.

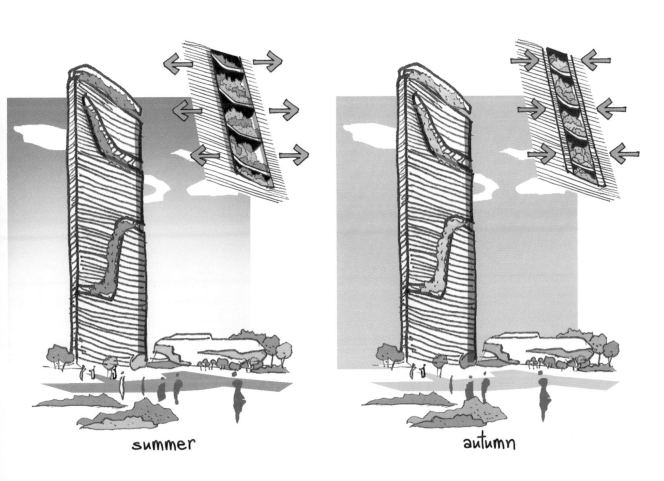

summer   autumn

While recognizing that in addressing environmental decline the most vital and pressing issue that all designers must address in their work today. This concerns not just those in the design field but all of society in all fields of work and study.

Simply stated, green design——or ecodesign—— is about harmonizing everything that humans make and do with nature. Achieving a resilient future is not just about changing our built environment, its systems, and their design. The change must start with humans as the predominant specie. We need to change our attitude to nature and change all of our acts in nature so we are not voracious exploiters of it, but guardians.

Silent Spring

We need to re-examine and change how our human society globally lives, works, carries out our activities, builds, and uses our urban developments. Our industrial economies, <u>food production</u> systems, <u>businesses</u>, <u>industrial</u>

systems, <u>mobility and movement</u> systems, <u>society</u>, and <u>social</u> and <u>political</u> systems need to be shaped with consideration of the

natural environment. We need to respond to these even though these areas require

radical societal change that is beyond the realm of the designer.

We need to recognize that we still have a long way to go toward achieving this ideal. If we look at nature, we will find that its only source of energy is from the sun. So if we want to be truly ecological in our architecture, its only main source of energy should be from the 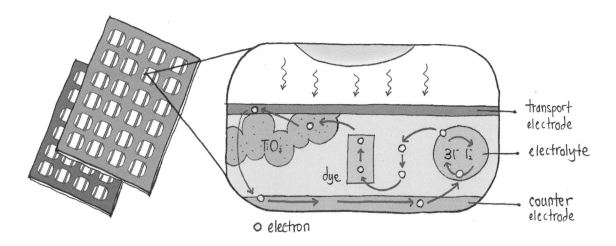 . But how do we get all the energy that society needs today for our built environment from the sun?

○ electron

photovoltaic dye-cell systems

Presently we use photovoltaics (for "high grade" energy production) and thermal solar collectors (for "low grade" energy production), but their efficiencies are still low. There are, of course, new technologies being developed, such as

photovoltaic dye-cell systems that partially imitate the

photosynthetic process, or artificial photosynthesis, but it will be some time before these achieve a commercially viable level of efficiency.

I contend that the truly green building is presently non-existent and has yet to be designed and built. No one has yet achieved this ideal, and it will be some time before anyone designs the truly ecomimetic built system. The totally green building is presently too exorbitant to build, and requires significant research and development work on its ecomimetic attributes, technological systems, and theoretical, interpretive, and design integration advancements. What we have today is a green built environment that approximates a certain level of environmental resilience, as "shades" of greenness, but not in totality.

What is distressing is the arrogance of many architects who contend that they have all the solutions to ecoarchitecture. I believe that nobody has all the technical answers to designing a totally green building. We still have a long way to go.

restore

enhance

In summary, my work is about addressing environmental issues by designing to redress and restore what human beings have callously done to the natural environment, and then seeking ways to build to enable humans to live and carry out activities in harmony with nature. Our design is not just to eliminate or reduce our constructional and operational negative consequences, but should be design done to positively contribute to the existing natural environment so that net gains enhance the ecological nexus and biodiversity, enhancing the provision of ecosystem services and other environmental benefits.

As mentioned earlier, a significant aspect of the negative environmental impairment caused by our built environment could have been averted by our anticipatory pre-design into buildings before they were built. Ecodesign's objective is then anticipatory—to design to achieve the reduction and eventual elimination of any negative impact at the outset of design inasmuch as possible prior to construction or production. Knowing what could constitute potential environmentally hazardous outcomes at the design stage becomes a crucial factor in green design.

Of course significant energy and water cost savings can be achieved in green buildings that amortize the initial additional financial premium needed to achieve a high green rating over 4–5 years. Resultant energy and water savings further contribute to reducing

the usual commercial "service charges" payable by the building's tenants. These savings justify only part of the "business case" for green buildings.

Studies by real estate agents show that a green building tends to appreciate in value higher and faster then non-green buildings that are "energy and water guzzling". Ultimately however, the case for green building and for designing for environmental resilience is not by commercial justifications, but is an ethical issue that our responsible human society must address.

Unfortunately, many investors who want green architecture are acutely concerned with the additional premium for greening. For many investors today, their key concerns are speed — how fast can we deliver the building — and cost — how cheaply the building can be delivered. <u>For many it is still not truly about the ethics of greening.</u> In practice, this premium decreases with the high-end buildings where the higher development budget permits greater opportunities for greening.

I found that many architects who are not conversant with ecodesign, are essentially designing buildings in the same way that they had been conventionally doing all along, and then get the M&E (Mechanical and Electrical) engineers to make their designs green by technological compliance to the tick boxes of an accreditation system such as LEED. Upon receiving a LEED rating, they then claim that their buildings are indeed green. This is the downside of these accreditation systems.

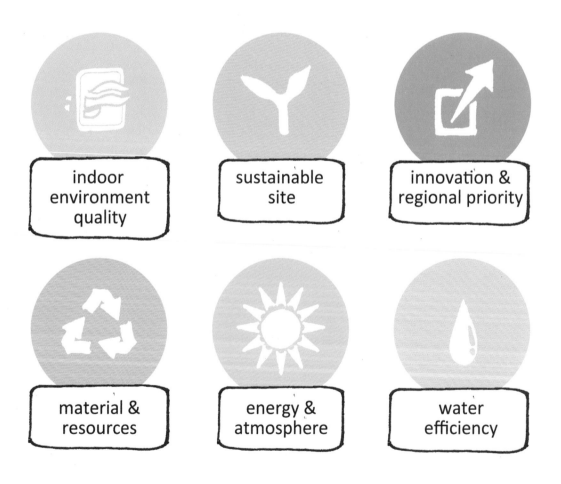

indoor environment quality

sustainable site

innovation & regional priority

material & resources

energy & atmosphere

water efficiency

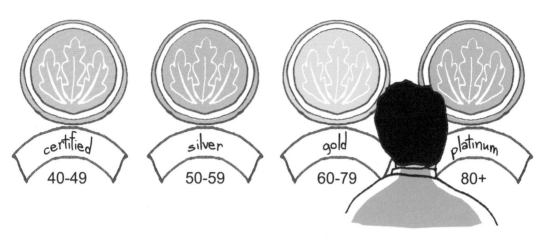

certified 40-49   silver 50-59   gold 60-79   platinum 80+

I see certification systems <u>as an index.</u> It is a common denominator for a group of buildings that focus essentially on green technology and ecoengineering. A LEED-rated building's green certification is not reflected in its aesthetics. A LEED Platinum building can look simply ugly. It can be totally dysfunctional. It is disconnected from its ecological context, and can be inhumane to occupy or use. One might question how certification can be regarded as green without any consideration given to biointegration with the ecology of the land?

What we get are buildings that are essentially engineering-driven, and stuffed with all types of eco-technologies, "a gadget architecture," without any consideration given to their probable high embodied energy content and to the environmental biology and climate of the locality. Many rating systems mislead architects and the public into thinking that if the architect achieves a high rating, or stuffs the building with enough ecoengineering systems (solar collectors, photovoltaic cells, wind generators, mechanical waste treatment systems, etc.) the outcome is an instantly green building. Nothing is of course further from the truth.

The resultant built structure remains, essentially, mostly inorganic with excessive technology, and usually has overly high embodied energy content because of its excessive engineering systems needed to compensate for its non-bioclimatically responsive built forms or plan forms. Many may also have excessively gratuitous, iconic features giving them an even higher level of embodied energy content and excessive (and wasteful) material content. The outcome is not ecoarchitecture. This is probably the most common misconception about ecodesign.

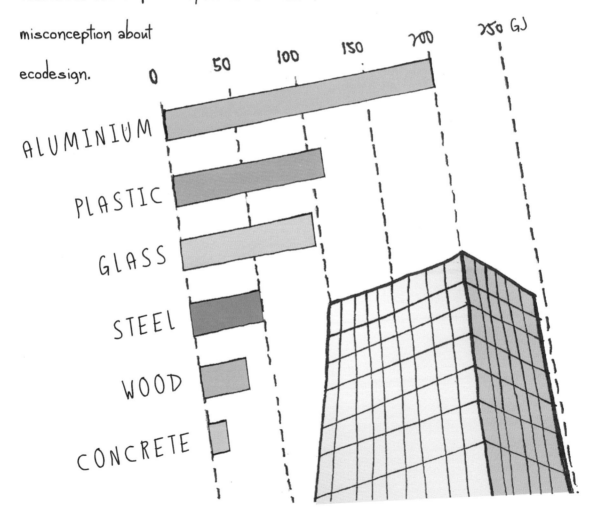

As mentioned earlier, I see ecoarchitecture as demanding a different way of designin — now with nature and its processes in mind. The design challenge is to finding the appropriate design solution that biointegrates all four sets of ecoinfra structure into a whole to achieve as deep a level of physical and systemic biointegration as possible.

CONSTRUCTED WETLAND FOR WATER TREATMENT AND PURIFICATION

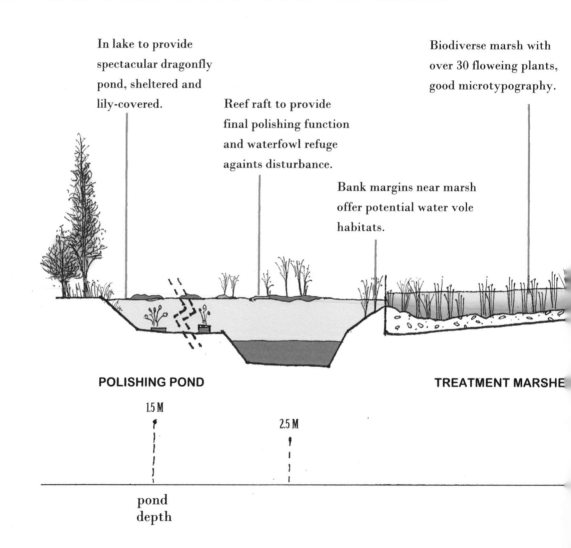

In lake to provide spectacular dragonfly pond, sheltered and lily-covered.

Reef raft to provide final polishing function and waterfowl refuge againts disturbance.

Biodiverse marsh with over 30 floweing plants, good microtypography.

Bank margins near marsh offer potential water vole habitats.

POLISHING POND

TREATMENT MARSHE

1.5 M

2.5 M

pond depth

This is the goal of ecodesign, which is the prime focus of all my work.

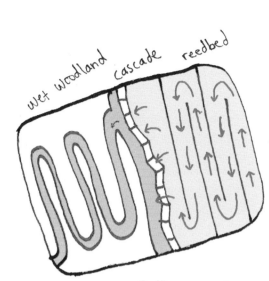

wet woodland   cascade   reedbed

Wet woodland channels to be no less than 150cm wide, no wider than 400cm. Wet woodland with creek developed three-tier structure. Phased introdution of ground flora. From marsh to shade tolerant species of damp soils.

Baffles approx. 1m apart 1m deep in a continuous zig zag.

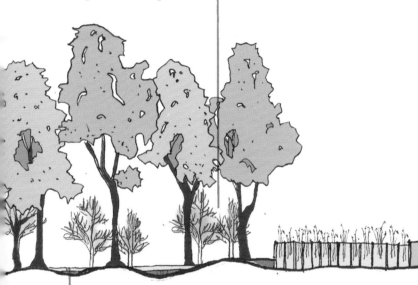

Normal water depth 100-150mm, occasional 300mm only with deeper ponds.

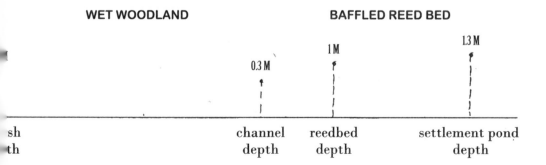

WET WOODLAND   **BAFFLED REED BED**

                0.3 M   1 M   1.3 M

sh
th   channel   reedbed   settlement pond
                depth   depth   depth

24%

ECOMIM

ECO

My research work led to the proposition of ecodesign as the design of our built environment to become living systems and constructed ecosystems, which require

PHYSICAL & SYSTEMIC BIOINTEGRATION

of hydrological, ecological, engineering, and societal

ECOINFRASTRUCTURES

into a whole.

DESIGN

issue 007

Achieving this seamlessly with net positive benefits to the natural environment (opposed to creating further negative consequences) is the challenge of ecodesign. The design task in my daily work is to find appropriate solutions to achieve this goal.

My daily work in centered around four R's — the first two R's are "Reading" and "Riting." Being a compulsive reader, I read just about everything and anything in front of me, but more specifically I read to research this field of endeavor. I write to proselytize the ideas and get feedback. The third R is "Rithmetic," which is essentially making the business of architecture commercially viable. The forth R is what drives my day, "Rchitecture," the interpretation of my research work in the design and execution of ecoarchitecture and eco-masterplans to the best of my ability.